An Autobiography of Life on the Road By a 60's / 70's Touring Musician

Martin Woodward

Acknowledgements

To all the fantastic musicians who I've had the privilege of working with back in the 1960s / 70s including:

Pip Williams (guitarist / record producer); Tex Marsh (drums); Roger Flavell (bassist / singer / songwriter); Kevan Fogarty (guitarist); Tommy Hunt (singer); Ron Thomas (bassist); Martin Johnstone (bassist / vocals); Keith Suckling (drums); Alan Griffin (guitarist); Tony Hall (saxophonist); Brent Scott Carter (saxophonist); Geno Washington (singer); UK No. 1 singer / songwriter Emile Ford; U.K. top 10 artists: *'The Fantastics'* - John Cheatdom; Jerome Ramos; Donald Haywoode and Richard Pitts.

To the other members of *'Aquila'*:

Ralph Denyer (singer / songwriter); Phil Childs (bassist); Jim Smith (drums); George Lee (saxophonist).

To my early mentors:

Alan Simonds (guitarist / vocalist); big bruv Steve (guitarist) and Mr. Henley (my inspirational music teacher at Warlingham School 1960 - 65).

Contents

Introduction

I've no doubt that every touring musician from every era has incredible stories to tell and they will of course all be vastly different. Sadly, most will go unwritten and lost forever.

Here's my story which includes the following highlights:

- The price of being the rookie
- The German US / UK bases
- 23 gigs in one week
- Travelling back in time
- The incredible NATO base in Naples
- The plane that caught fire mid flight
- The villa from Hell
- 3 in a bed
- Deported from Spain
- The Piper Club Rome
- 24 hours stranded in the Alps with no heater
- Nightmare in Paris
- Lulu's party
- Signed to RCA
- Gigs with Elton John, Bowie and others

- The Paradiso club Amsterdam
- A conversation with André Previn
- Life gets easy
- An incredible coincidence
- Me the Snake and the snow
- A gig with Buddy Rich
- A life changing decision
- Bring on the strippers
- Mouflon spotting in Cyprus
- The re-unions

You've no doubt heard people going on about the good old days and may think that it's just old fogeys going senile. Well, I can assure you that so much really was better then. Ok we didn't have all the amazing technology that's around today. No mobile phones, no computers and cars were much more basic and less reliable, but much easier to fix. *And cost a hell of a lot less to buy in the first place!*

But what we did have was real freedom and everything seemed safer and certainly less corrupt. Many things were much better and most people grew up respecting their elders. Kids could play out safely and it was normal for kids to walk to school alone or with their mates.

Sometimes on our way home from our school Winston Churchill would drive passed in his Rolls Royce on his way home to Chartwell. We'd all stand and salute him and he'd give us his famous 'V for victory' sign. *Well, I think it was that sign anyway!*

At seven years old I used to walk to my piano lessons alone in the dark with only occasional lampposts. Curiously my main fear was the dark and ghosts but I never actually saw any. I was never worried about people even though there were dodgy people about even then, but thankfully I never came across any.

But there were downsides, schools were far stricter than they are now. If you stepped out of line you got the cane. But I managed to avoid it although I have to say some of the teachers were out and out bullies and I can think of a couple that I'd like to string up - *but most were great!* However, I did get quite a few pastings from my father. I could never quite understand him when he used to say, "This is hurting me far more than it's hurting you!" I thought, "No it's bloody not!" But actually, they didn't do me any harm. Even Dennis the Manace used to end up getting a pasting at the end of every comic strip until the stupid *'woke'* brigade moved in and turned an iconic character into pathetic wimp.

Overall things were much better and it was a much happier world to live in. I remember my childhood prime minister, Harold McMillan saying "You've never had it so good!" And he was right, the war was over, rationing had ended and there was full employment where a man could earn enough on a single wage to pay a mortgage and keep his family decently. It was the exception that mothers would go to work and when they did it created a nice surplus for the family income - our mother never went out to work after my brother's and I were born.

Furniture and electrical goods were major purchases back then and were made to last and be repaired rather than dumped and replaced. I must have been over 10 years old before we had a fridge and a washing machine, and throughout my childhood and teens we only ever had three TV's and none were colour. I remember our father bringing home our first TV ready to watch the coronation in 1953 and just plonked it in the middle of the floor as there were no designated places for TVs then. There was only one channel - BBC, although ITV followed soon after, but you had to buy another set for that - which we didn't get for a few years. The first programme I ever saw was Noddy - which was written, watched, and enjoyed in total innocence, then the woke brigade moved in and censored it - *pathetic!*

History is as it was and shouldn't be re-written to suit present day opinions. Yeh, sure a lot of history may have been crap, but re-writing it doesn't make it better, *it just exposes the people who do it to be a bunch of liars!*

We were one of a minority of families who had central heating, but only as my father was able to do it himself. And very few families owned a car, although we did. Parking was rarely an issue back then, even in London there were some free places to park. But now as soon as you stop just about anywhere someone will have their hand out to fleece you.

And of course, in those days, shops were closed on Sundays, which made it a day for church and / or family picnics etc.

Sorry, I could go on and on about life in the past, but that's not what this book is about.

The Music Beginning

For me I guess it all began in about 1962 when my elder brother Steve bought an electric guitar. He practiced almost constantly and it wasn't long before he could knock out a few Shadows tunes - which we were both into very much, just like most of the teenagers of that era.

We used to listen to radio Luxembourg every night without fail (MW 208), deep into the night on our transistor radios - *'tranny's'* as they were called then. Later the word *'tranny'* referred to a Transit van, and still later has yet another meaning - *no offence intended!* And in a few years, it may mean something else again. It's quite frightening how words can change their meanings over the years and often cause unintended offence. In fact, some nursery rhymes we were taught as five-year-olds could now get you locked up!

As I took piano lessons from a fairly young age, I was able to accompany Steve on the piano. Although not brilliant it wasn't too bad - *actually, it was probably bloody awful, but I don't remember it as being too bad!*

Our first live performance was at our local Methodist church which life largely revolved around. Well, it seemed to go fairly well, although throwing things and shouting abuse wasn't the done thing for a church congregation, they probably just gritted their teeth, clapped politely and prayed for our improvement; but we were definitely lacking a few other musicians.

Inevitably it wasn't long before we wanted to start a group. We had a mate called Charlie Barker who also had a guitar and limited ability and another mate called Eric Williams who had a bass guitar. But we were short of a drummer. So, Steve (who was working and had an income) bought me a snare drum and a high hat. We didn't have enough money to get a bass drum, and tom toms etc.

Well, I had no idea how to play the drums (or drum) but we practiced and practiced until Charlie Barker's dad said we were as good as the Shadows, probably in the hope that we'd stop practicing in his lounge. Eventually we did our first unpaid gig at the local Methodist youth club which was a total disaster and we were booed off stage - *the youth club crowd weren't quite as forgiving as the church lot!*

Clearly playing the *'drum'* was not my forte. And although a piano was not an option due to the transportation problem, a portable organ clearly was right up my street, but sadly they were out of my price range (with me still being at school and having no income), This temporarily put an end to things for me.

But Steve secured a position as bass player with a great local band called Sounds Anonymous, the leader of whom worked with Steve at the Vox amplifier factory. His name was Alan Simonds who became a lifelong friend. The first time I went to one of their rehearsals I was totally blown away. I remember they did 'Pretty Woman', 'Under the boardwalk' and several songs by the 'Stones'. By this time things had moved on considerably with groups like the Beatles, the Animals, the Yardbirds, the Kinks, the Zombies, the Graham Bond Organization, the Moody Blues etc. It was a whole new exciting era, which I'm so privileged to have lived through.

I remember going to one of Sounds Anonymous's gigs at one of the local Saturday morning cinemas when they had a brilliant stand in lead guitarist called Alan Griffin who played with another local group called the Subjects. Much later I played with Alan Griffin with Geno Washington.

A little later Alan Simonds bought a Farfisa organ. I walked a 16-mile round trip to his house just to see it - there were no bus routes and it was Sunday anyway. My desire to acquire an organ was totally intense. But although the Farfisa was good and became iconic, I wanted a Vox Continental as used by the Animals, the Doors, and many others at the time.

As life progressed a little further, while still at school I got a part time job in Sainsbury's in Selsdon - before they were a self-service supermarket. There were two long counters either side of the shop split into four sections: groceries and dairy one side, and cooked meats and butchers the other side. This of course was way before decimal currency when we had the good old pounds, shillings, and pence. Everything anyone bought had to be totted up on a piece of paper - far more complicated than today's shops.

The income from Sainsbury's enabled me to convince my father to lend me the £200 necessary to purchase my Vox Continental - there was no hire purchase allowed in our house! This forged the real beginning for me.

Not long after we formed a group called the Element with Steve on guitar, Martin Tottle (who I worked with at Sainsbury's) on bass, a friend of his called Bill Martin on guitar and Keith Suckling the drummer from the then disbanded Sounds Anonymous. Alan Simonds was the manager, coordinator, and argument resolver - *Steve and I used to argue almost constantly!*

The Element on stage - No idea where! Probably 1964/65.

We did lots of Animal's material and also quite a few Beach Boys songs. It was certainly much better than our previous efforts but still nowhere near professional. Even so we regularly played at the local youth clubs for a few quid. Another group who did the same circuit incidentally was 'Mud' who later became very famous.

L-R - Steve, Bill, Keith, Martin (Tottle), Me (on Vox organ)

Not sure how or why the Element ended, but after that I played with a few local semi-pro bands, then joined a half descent semi-pro band called Philby's 5 who had lots of regular gigs all around London. By this time, I'd left school and was working in a music publisher just off Dean Street in London. During the time with Philby's 5, I made enough money to pay off my organ debt. But it was hard working by day and gigging by night and something had to give, so I left Philby's 5 and stopped gigging for a while.

Once turned 17 I passed my driving test thanks to my dad teaching me. This of course was incredibly useful.

Commuting to the West End every day from South Croydon was a pain and took up over three hours of each day. So, I then left the music publisher and got a job as a counter assistant (or P&TO as they were officially called) in Croydon Post Office which was a much easier commute. This enabled me to continue as a semi pro musician in various local bands. But I'd outgrown the Vox Continental and wanted a Hammond which cost £1500. To put this in perspective you could buy a house in South London at this time for about £4000. So, the Hammond was one hell of a cost.

For months I went around all the music shops in and around London to play them. I had all the brochures which I used to fall asleep reading. Unknowingly I was performing a very powerful visualisation / actualisation mental exercise which later resulted in my father lending me the money to buy a second-hand Hammond M102 as used by Procol Harum, Georgie Fame, Alan Price, Keith Emerson and many others by then. Actually, Keith Emerson used a Hammond L100 but you'd never know the difference! The Hammonds were built like tanks, *which was just as well with what Keith Emerson used to do to his!*

I also got a small van which my father kitted out so that I could transport my Hammond and speakers easily. But I was deeply in debt.

Tapestry

By then it was 1968 and I was in demand as organists were gold dust especially if they had a Hammond. I was approached by a school friend Mike Hutson who was with a band called Tapestry who had a record contract with Nems records. Their producer was Pete Gage who was the guitarist and originator of Geno Washington and the Ram Jam band. He clearly knew his stuff. At the time he was living with singer Elkie Brooks in Downham, near Bromley, they later married and further down the line divorced.

The pressure was on for me to pack up working in the post office and join them with no guarantees of a regular income which my father was not happy about.

Anyway, I took the plunge and so that we could rehearse in the afternoons, Mike and I took part-time jobs at Gatwick airport cleaning in the early mornings. I also had a gig on my own playing at the Swan and Sugar loaf, South Croydon on Friday and Saturday evenings.

The other members of Tapestry when I joined were: Mike Hutson (vocals) David Moses (bass), and John (Chic) Webb (drums). But initially we were short of a guitarist so advertised for one in the Melody Maker. A few came to the audition but only two of significance. One was Pip Williams who was totally amazing - world class and blew us all away, but he didn't take the job as he was earning regular money with the Fantastics. But he nevertheless kept in touch with me and Mike and he was later to become very prominent in my life. The other guitarist was Pete Frolich who ironically, I had previously played with in a local band called the Images and he got the job. Although Pete wasn't in Pip's league, he was very good.

Not long after, Pete Gage came up with a song that had been written by two members of the Dakotas, Robin McDonald and Mick Green called 'Heart and Soul' and instigated a professional orchestral arrangement by Richard Hewson which we later recorded. Elkie Brook's brother, Tony Mansfield was the Dakotas drummer, so I guess that's possibly where the connection came from.

At the recording session Mike (who was the singer) was a great deal miffed as Pete Gage decided last moment that Pete Frolich the guitarist should sing lead on it. In retrospect it was the right decision, no disrespect to Mike.

It ended up being a very well-made pop song, got stacks of air play and was Alan Freeman's tip for the top. Alan Freeman was the top radio / TV DJ at the time!

We didn't do many live gigs, but I do remember we once worked at a private function in Madame Tussauds (waxworks). When we were playing, I had Henry IV peering over my shoulder - *I guess this was the only time I ever played to royalty!*

L-R - Chick, Me, Pete, David, Mike.
Sorry about the quality of the photo but it seems to be the only image that has survived!

Later Mike and I crept down into the *'out of bounds'* chamber of horrors in the dark with a torch - *spooky!* Another live gig we did was BBC Radio London with Elton John. All was going great - then the bloody record company went bust! Well, that was one hell of a blow and the end of Tapestry as it was.

So next I formed a trio with Alan Simonds on bass and Keith the drummer from Sounds Anonymous. That was going very nicely and we got a few gigs, but not enough to earn a living.

3 offers in 1 day!

Then out of the blue Pip Williams phoned up and asked me if I could take my Hammond round to his parents' house in West Drayton with view to joining the new band that he was forming for the Fantastics.

Later that same day I got an offer to join a working pro band in Brighton and an offer also came in for me, Keith and Alan to work on a cruise ship to Australia for six months.

I must admit that I was torn between the cruise and the Fantastics, but I could see that the Fantastics would be the most sensible stepping stone to better things, but it was sad to leave my mates.

The Fantastics

The Fantastics were a black US soul group like the Temptations and we were the backing band and took the name of Tapestry which was then redundant. The Fantastics later had a top 10 hit with 'Something Old, Something New' which is regularly played at weddings. Previously in the US they'd had a No. 1 hit but they were then called the Veleurs.

After my initial get together with Pip where we ran through the Fantastics set list, I met the other members, Jim and Ronnie when we had a full rehearsal at Jerry's flat in London - *Jerry was one of the Fantastics*. Shortly after, we did our first gig at the Lyceum with the Move where I had the privilege of meeting Roy Wood (of the Move, ELO and Wizard), who was a lovely man.

LYCEUM
STRAND · W.C.2.
WEDNESDAY 19th MARCH 1969
7·30 - MIDNIGHT
GUEST D. J.'s plus
THE MOVE AND THE FANTASTICS
68 DISC DATE
TICKETS
ADVANCE 10/-
available from any
MECCA BALLROOM
or at the door 12's

The band members were me on organ, Pip on guitar, Ronnie Thomas on bass and Jim Smith on drums. The others were all older than me and seasoned veterans having all previously played in numerous professional bands. *So, I was the rookie which came with a price!*

One of Jim's previous bands was the London Beats who were the first Western group to play behind the Iron Curtain, mainly Poland, which is where he met his wife, Myja. In Poland Jim was stupidly rich, but unfortunately all the money he made was worthless on the foreign exchange market. He changed what he could on the black market, as well as smuggling out gold and jewellery. He also had a stack of grief bringing his wife home. When Myja finally escaped to the West, she couldn't understand why Jim wasn't being mobbed in the street as he would have been in Poland! Jim then later played with the Nashville Teens.

Pip Williams in his early days.

Pip had previously toured extensively with Jimmy Ruffin and a London band called the Sovereigns as well as the previous Fantastic's band Clockwork Orange.

Ronnie had also played with numerous pro bands; I know Hamilton's Movement was one of them. His party trick was to lay on the floor, stick his legs over his head and light his farts which went off like a flame thrower. *How he never accidentally blew his nuts off is a mystery!*

The Fantastics L-R Jerry, Richie, Don & John

The Fantastics were Don Haywoode, John Cheatdom, Jerry Ramos (aka Romy) and Richard Pitts. The great thing about joining them was that I had a regular income with all hotel expenses paid which I badly needed to reduce my huge organ debt.

Well, what a lad Jerry was. His flat was full of women! One sleeping in the bath, some in the hallway others in the lounge, others in the kitchen - I never went in the bedroom but I'd have been surprised if it was empty! As I was to find out later, he'd meet girls at gigs and then after an initial grooming in his hotel room they were invited to live with him in London all assuming that they were the only one - hence the harem. Ultimately, they'd eventually all get the message and go home.

But actually, underneath his crazy facade of drinking, fighting, gambling, and womanising, Jerry was a lovely man - *a bit like Rasputin!* He once came into my room unannounced when I was reading the bible which I quickly hid under the pillow. But he said, "No, no, no man, there's no shame in reading the good book, you carry on." Back in those days there was a Gideons bible in every hotel or guest house bedroom! I did try reading it right the way through as it undoubtedly contains much wisdom, but there's an awful lot of sex and violence in there too!

Don was living with his long-time girlfriend Marion who later turned out to be a bit of a mother figure. Marion was from Bradford and was allegedly the first black girl to arrive there. I assume she was adopted but never asked her. Don was without doubt the calmest of all of them and if I had to pick a favourite it would probably be him, although they were all very different and I liked all of them.

John had a long-time girlfriend who was one of the Flirtations (group). She used to confuse me as she had numerous wigs and I always thought John was with different women. Richard was a bit of a lad like Jerry but not quite as wild.

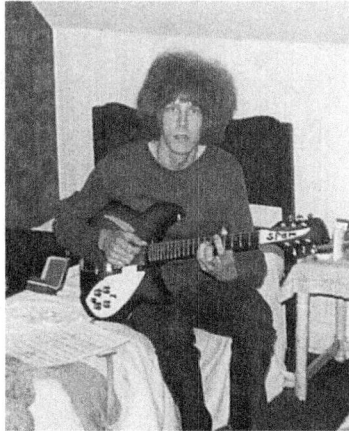

Spam!

Peter Cole aka Spam was the Fantastics' driver and valet. He also became a good friend. He had a lot to contend with as the Fantastics used to argue with one another virtually constantly and occasionally beat shit out of one another whilst they were being driven on the motorway. If a white guy ever used the language they used on one another even in jest, they'd be locked up for racism ten times over. I wouldn't feel comfortable repeating what they used to call one another for fear of reprisals.

For the first few gigs we didn't have a van or road manager but hired the services of a couple of guys called Dick and

Ian who had a Transit van. Ian turned out to be Ian Hunter of 'Mott the Hoople' which he was forming at the time. I remember our second gig was at the 400 Ballroom in Torquay which was a fair trek for a one-night stand. For much of the return journey the others fell asleep, but I stayed awake talking to Ian who was driving. He told me his stories of when he worked the Hamburg scene with the Beatles - he was then with a band called Freddie Fingers Lee. He obviously knew the Beatles very well. He also told me that he was finally relieved at finding his true musical identity with the band that he was then forming (Mott). Ian was 10 years older than me.

After the gigs he did with us the next time I met Ian was in the Marquee club when I was with Aquila and Mott was going strong. Funnily enough he was behind me talking to someone else and I recognised his very prominent Liverpudlian voice and called his name before I even saw him. We had a good chat and he told me of a great new band on the scene called Genesis! Ian gave me his phone number and suggested we keep in touch, but I never spoke to him again. He was a great guy and I'm so glad he was successful!

Stonehenge

Anytime we were returning from the west country in the early mornings we would always pass Stonehenge. At that time there was no fence around it, you could just pull in there and do what you liked.

At 3:30 am in the summer just as the sun was beginning to rise it was a really mystical and eerie place. We would nearly always pull in there and jump around the stones - like the monkeys around the monolith in the film '2001 A Space Odyssey.' Mad? Well, we were mad! *We were also probably the reason they eventually fenced the place off!*

The Hotels

Wherever sensibly possible we would return to London after one night stands even as far away as Plymouth or Middlesbrough etc. So sometimes it could get quite tiring. Moreso for me as I was dropped off at our pickup point in London and then had another hour plus drive to Blindley Heath in Surrey. But on the plus side there were no speed limits on the trunk roads and motorways, no speed cameras, the roads were empty after midnight and Transits could do 100mph easily. Driving at night in those days was really pleasurable, especially on an empty motorway at 120mph! I remember one time I got from Sheffield to Ealing, West London in one hour and twenty-five minutes. I guess now the same journey would take four hours or more, depending on roadworks and / or accidents.

Often, I wouldn't get home till the morning rush hour started but fortunately I was going in the opposite direction. I'd just get settled in bed and the damn kid next door would start buzzing around his garden on his incredibly noisy petrol go cart!

Whenever there was a series of consecutive gigs in the same direction it obviously made sense to use hotels or similar. Sometimes, but not always the Fantastics would stay in a different hotel to us and we'd nearly always share a room. Mostly I'd share with Jim, but I did also share with Donald a few times too.

Most of the UK *'hotels'* or *'guest houses'* we stayed in with the Fantastics ranged from moderately ok to unbelievably crap. In fact, by today's standards, I doubt many would get licences as dog kennels. Before getting into bed, it was always wise to do a thorough inspection to see what might have got there first. But I have to say that I never got bitten by anything nasty or caught any horrible infection as a result of lousy accommodation.

Many of the bedrooms had electric heaters with coin meters. Fortunately, Jim knew a way to rig the meters so that we didn't have to pay anything. In fact, at his flat in London he had the electric meter running three weeks forwards and two weeks backwards. He did show me how to do this, but it was positively dangerous and not something I'd risk personally. *It probably wouldn't work these days as the meters are now more sophisticated than they used to be!*

He also had to make sure the wires were the right way round when the meter reader came. Apparently, on one reading, the figure was lower than the previous one. The meter reader just scratched his head and assumed that he'd made a mistake previously.

My first night away with the band was in Manchester when we stayed at a *'hotel'* (if you can call it that) above an Indian restaurant. No fear of any reprisals mentioning this as the place would have been condemned years ago. The place was an absolute dump. We all slept in the same large room in separate beds thank God and there was a wash basin in the corner which was used for all sorts! The toilets and showers were down a long dark corridor; en suites were a distant dream.

Another guest house I still have nightmares about was in Scarborough. The place was run by a big fat mama with black hairy legs, ok no problem there, but in the morning, I found a short black curly hair in my scrambled eggs. The worst thing was that I also found another one stuck between my teeth! *That put me off scrambled eggs for over a decade!*

The price of being the rookie

Immediately prior to the first night away, the others took a dislike to my shoes as they weren't trendy enough. So they decided to set fire to them - *whilst they were still on my feet!* They did this by igniting an aerosol which turned it into a flame thrower - *potentially incredibly dangerous!* The charred remains of my only pair of shoes got shoved into a letter box in Albert Square, Manchester, leaving me shoeless. - *That was the price of being the rookie!*

The next day which was heaving with rain they took me to a shoe shop and bought me a suitable pair of shoes. It was a bit embarrassing walking into a shoe shop with no shoes especially in the pouring rain so I had to pretend to be mentally subnormal - *which wasn't too difficult!*

All night cafes

Watford gap services (The Blue Boar) on the M1 was / is probably in the most strategic position of the whole motorway network, as it's right at the point where the traffic splits left to go to Birmingham, Manchester and the Northwest, or straight on for Nottingham, Sheffield, Leeds and the Northeast.

Consequently, when returning to London from the North (East or West) the Blue Boar was the last sensible stop off place and where we and most other bands always headed for. When we got there, I knew we were almost home (only another 100 miles). If you went to the Southbound section most nights between midnight and 3:00 am you would be virtually guaranteed to find travelling musicians on their way home. I guess this is the same now. But fifty years ago, the place had a reputation for paper plates, plastic cutlery, rubber sausages, greasy chips and always having a thumb dipped into the beans as they were being scooped out. It's no doubt improved somewhat now but the prices have also gone through the roof.

The Blue Boar was there in its strategic position even before the M1, which is why originally it became the only privately owned services on the motorway network. But since then, it's been bought out by the big boys - *hence the never-ending price hikes!*

Back in the day there were numerous all night transport cafes on all the trunk routes often frequented by musicians and lorry drivers in the middle of the night. I remember one on the A303 at Honiton which we used to frequent on the Plymouth route and another near Wakefield. They all had an atmosphere of their own helped on by the pin ball machines and the greasy cuisine. And there were also many town-centre all night kiosks / caravans like Greasy Vera's in Sheffield and many more in London and Manchester. It's very sad to see these places die out. I know you get the odd 24-hour McDonald's, but they're not the same - *they don't have souls!*

Weston-Super-Mare

After Dick and Ian Hunter departed, we hired a transit van for a while and had a temporary roadie called Roger. During this time, we once gigged at the Winter Gardens in Weston-Super-Mare.

At this gig a group of schoolgirls took a shine to me (our lads say that they must have been from the local blind school). And afterwards they started chasing me. Well, I'd never run as slowly in my life! When they inevitably caught me, they just wrote my name all over the van in lipstick which went down an absolute storm with the hire company.

An encounter with the village nutter

At one gig in Scarborough which was upstairs (probably the Scene One and Two), at the end of the evening when Roger the roadie was packing away, I asked him for the van keys as I'd left my cigarettes in there. After getting them I took the keys back and he asked me if I'd locked it which I hadn't, so I said I'd go back and do it. I didn't take the keys again as all you had to do was push the knobs down.

On my way down the stairs a huge mad guy grabbed hold of me by the throat and was shouting, "Fuzz, fuzz," as he pinned me up against the wall. Shortly after, Ronnie came down the stairs and as soon as this nutter saw him, he let go of me and went for him instead. Before he could get hold of him, I said, "Quick Ron get to the van!" So, we both made a dash for the van, got in and locked it before he got to us. But unfortunately, as I no longer had the keys we couldn't drive off. By then this guy was really mad and started bashing the side windows with his elbow and rocking the van around. As he was bashing one side, Ron and I moved over to the other side. Then he'd change sides. Then he calmed down and asked for a cigarette. We opened the window about a quarter of an inch and stuffed a load of cigarettes out. Then he went mad again and started bashing it again. Then he calmed down again and said, "Come on lads I'm not going to hurt you, just open the door." I said, "You go upstairs and get our road manager and we'll open the door." And believe it or not that's what he did - and Roger, who was bigger than him just told him to piss off!

When he'd got far enough away, Ron and I got out of the van and ran in the opposite direction. Shortly we found a Bobby on the beat (yes back in those days the police used to patrol the streets on foot) and told him what had happened. He said, "Oh that's only old Fuzz, come on let's go and sort him out!" I said, "We're not going back there with just you on your own mate, you better get some reinforcements." So, he reluctantly called for backup and we then walked back to the club at a safe distance. Later we saw him running down the stairs with a policeman's hat on and three policemen chasing him.

When I met Ron fifty years later, he'd got no recollection of this event at all, but I'm damn sure I didn't dream it. I guess, we all remember and forget different things over the years.

Ragarse the Roadie

After not too long we acquired a permanent roadie with his own Transit van nicknamed Ragarse. I know his real first name was John but unfortunately can't remember his surname name which is a shame as I'd love to find him, but I do remember that he was from Kidderminster. *If you're out there somewhere mate, please get in touch!* He got named Ragarse because his jeans were always hanging around his arse. More about him later.

Ragarse in Frankfurt - Picture courtesy of Pete Cole

More gigs

After the first few gigs the memories started merging into one. Basically, we were working every night with just the occasional night off, but I didn't mind as I loved it.

One particularly memorable gig for me was when we worked at Middlesbrough City Hall with the US band Three Dog Night and Pete Gage and Elkie Brooks came to see me. Pete knew that I was working with the Fantastics probably from Mike Hutson.

Pete was then working with Jimmy James and the Vagabonds and obviously also had a gig in or near Middlesbrough. They invited us all to a barbeque on the beach at Redcar afterwards but unfortunately, we had to get off.

Three Dog Night were a great bunch of lads and they let me use their Hammond B3 to save dragging mine in, they also gave me a long lecture about smoking which was a waste of breath. Pete gave me the run down on the B3 controls as I wasn't fully acquainted with them.

Three Dog Night had a UK No. 1 with a song called 'One'. They were a superb band but I was particularly impressed by their drummer who was incredible and had arms like a gorilla.

I did eventually give up smoking a few years later, but only after I did a bit of maths and realised that what I was spending on them was a mortgage - *so I gave up smoking and bought a house instead!* - That was certainly the most sensible thing I ever did both from the health and financial points of view.

23 gigs in one week

We also occasionally did cabaret clubs where we worked the same place for a week - easy work - *sometimes!* The Showboat Middlesbrough was one. But another time we did Wigan Casino, Bolton Casino and the Garrick in Leigh all the same week - three gigs a night and three lots of humping gear; but on the last two nights we also drove across the Snake Pass to add Sheffield University to the list, then on the final night drove home to London and then for me onto Blindley Heath. That was one of the hardest weeks I ever did and we didn't get paid a bean more for it! *But we had to take the rough with the smooth!*

An out of body experience

During that week whilst staying in the Bolton digs, I had an out of body experience. Possibly this was brought about because of the stress due to the workload. I remember laying in my bed too tired to sleep (in a room that I was sharing with Jim, although I believe all the others were also in the room at the time) and from where I was laying, I couldn't see the window as it was an attic room with a beam in the way. The next moment I was looking out of the window and thought, "That's weird I can't see the window," then I turned around and saw myself laying on the bed. Then almost instantly I zoomed straight back into my body.

Me messing with Spam's guitar in a Bolton Hotel

Fifty years later when we had a reunion with Ronnie and Jim. They both said that I wanted to jump out of the window thinking I could fly and they all had to hold me down, but I have no memory of this at all. Well, I know it sounds like a drug related incident, but I certainly hadn't knowingly taken anything. I have incidentally had several out of body experiences since so I know I'm not mad!

Germany & Switzerland

Then one day the Fantastics said, "Right lads we're off to Germany in two days, get your passports ready." Well, I didn't have one; but miraculously my father ran round and got it sorted for me within 24 hours, something that you could never do now and it was pretty much unheard of even then.

So off we went to Frankfurt via Ostend through the middle of Brussels which was horrendous (from the driving point of view), but Jim being a veteran knew the way. Here the accommodation was much better than anywhere we stayed in the UK - incredibly clean and spacious. I was also overwhelmed by the department stores, the cake shops, the motorways, and the automat machines in the subways. You could get anything from a bar of chocolate to a teddy bear in those machines; and it was also quite entertaining to watch them operate.

The motorway system even then was more advanced than ours is now and much of it was built before the war. But the first thing that struck me was this place called 'Ausfahrt'. I thought this place must be huge as just about every junction leads there. Well, I twigged eventually - now of course you'd just Google it, *but you couldn't then!*

The pastry shops were out of this world. I used to go to one most mornings for a cake breakfast - *pity they couldn't make a decent pot of tea to go with it!*

There were also many other things I hadn't seen before like:

- Continental quilts - before they became common place in the UK, sheets and blankets were the norm. When I first saw these, I was horrified but soon got used to them

- Trams - they were everywhere. At that time the only remaining UK trams were in Blackpool

- Plastic carrier bags. I guess few people will remember the old paper carrier bags we used to use which were very much more ecofriendly; but every time you put one down in the wet the bottom would fall out and all your oranges would go rolling down the hill. These original plastic carrier bags didn't have the now compulsory air holes in them so that you couldn't suffocate your sproggs. As a result, they also made excellent water bombs which didn't take us long to discover

- Getting used to looking left first when crossing a road. In fact, I came very close to being flattened by a tram on several occasions and one time I got

> pulled back by a policeman and fined 10 Deutsch
> Marks for jaywalking

I can't remember how long we stayed on this first trip as the days and nights merged together. We were working the British / US army / air force bases. Every night we worked at least two gigs, some nights more, and there was always a long drive in-between and of course all the gear had to be humped in and out of these places and as we only had one road manager, we all had to assist which was not easy going - *especially humping my Hammond!*

On the plus side at many of the US bases we got a free T bone steak! How many bases there were I've no idea, but there must have been a hell of a lot as we never worked the same one twice. The US ones incidentally were much better than the British ones! And at most there was more than one club - one for the officers and another for the squaddies. The British officer's clubs were like proper nightclubs and the ones for the squaddies were like canteens. All the US ones were good, but some of the officers' clubs were amazing - like plush cabaret clubs.

For transportation in Germany, we had the Transit and two Mercedes limos. The mercs did 140mph and the Transit only did just over 100mph. Most of the time I travelled in the Transit to keep Ragarse awake. And I have to say there were a few times I had to grab the wheel and poke him in the ribs. Often, we'd be driving along at 100mph and massive juggernauts with huge trailers would overtake us at about 120mph or more - *really frightening when you were half asleep and didn't see them coming!*

Due to the dramatic speed difference the rest of the lads always got to the gigs and back to the hotel before me and Ragarse. One night when arriving back at the hotel shattered as usual, as I got out of the van, I felt a heavy thump on the back of my neck followed by a soaking feeling going right down my body. In that moment I thought I'd been hit by a tram and it was blood running down from my severed head. After realising that I wasn't dead and my head was still in place, I looked up to see Pip's laughing face from one of the upper hotel windows. *I'd been water bombed!*

One time a few of us were in the van going somewhere and as Ragarse pulled out of the parking bay he clipped the car in front breaking its rear light cluster. Ragarse decided to drive on despite us all suggesting he should stop. But another local motorist who saw what happened decided to chase us. So, we were darting through Frankfurt trying to lose this guy. As we jumped a few red lights a couple of police cars then joined in. We were eventually caught and dragged off to the local police station, where the other motorist told them what happened. We denied it and said the other guy was trying to kill us and we were trying to escape. We were then taken back to the scene of the incident, but the original car had gone and there was no trace of what happened, (apparently one of the others who remained at the hotel swept up the evidence), so they took the other guy away!

Towards the end of this trip. we flew out to West Berlin for a couple of days to work some more bases. This of course was when Germany and Berlin were split in two and the *'Berlin Wall'* was in place. I was amazed at how big West Berlin was as there was a fair distance between the gigs. We were staying in the centre in a really nice hotel (for once). But there was an air of depression about the place left over from the war, i.e., bullet holes in the sides of many of the buildings. I'm sure it's all different now. Then on the final day we did two gigs in the afternoon, flew back to Frankfurt, drove on to goodness knows where and then did two more gigs in the evening - *hard going!*

Travelling back in time

After a few more gigs we flew out from Frankfurt to Zurich for a gig at the Blackout club with a group called the Gun, who had a UK hit with 'Race with the Devil'. We stopped a night, then flew back to Heathrow. Although I'd been to Switzerland a few times it was mainly passing through. But Zurich was the first large Swiss city I'd ever been to. The two things that always impress me about Switzerland are, one the air quality and two the cleanliness. In fact, I remember having a cold when we left Frankfurt which cleared up immediately when we arrived in Zurich. Also, the women are incredibly tall - *must be all the fresh air!*

We left Zurich at 9:00 am and arrived back in Heathrow at 8:50 am ten minutes before we left which I thought was pretty cool and made me feel a bit like Dr Who; but then it took me six hours to get back to Blindley Heath via public transport. Meanwhile Ragarse was driving the gear back on his own ready for the next round of gigs.

The UK gigs then recommenced for a short while before we were off again, but the next trip was going to be a long one as the Fantastics could no longer work in the UK for six months due to work permit regulations. As a result of this sadly Ronnie decided to leave the band. So, Spam agreed to take over on bass - he'd previously played guitar and bass in several bands.

Germany, Italy, France & Majorca

So off we went again via Dover - Ostend, through Brussels again and onto Frankfurt. I completely lost count of how many bases we worked at in Germany but then came a gig in Naples at the NATO base for a few days. I remember exactly when this was as we changed planes in Milan when they were showing live pictures of the moon landing on big screens in the airport - 20th July 1969.

Meanwhile Ragarse had to spend two days driving through Austria and almost the full length of Italy with all the gear and Marion and one of the other girls who were not happy. They'd tried to get some of us (me probably) to give up their plane seats for them, but the Fantastics insisted that we all needed to arrive fresh for the gig. When they arrived the day after us, they looked like a bunch of dead dogs!

The hotel in Naples was superb and only a short walk from the base. The only problem was crossing one road which took about 15 minutes due to the nutty Italian drivers. Then when arriving at the base barrier we had to get security passes which only lasted for so many hours, so we had to repeat this complicated procedure each day, sometimes even twice a day - *'Jobsworths' taken to the extreme!*

That was also the first time I'd ever seen a watermelon man - I knew the song but didn't know that they really existed - *so refreshing in all that heat!*

The NATO officers club where we were working was out of this world, right on a cliff top overlooking the bay out towards the Isle of Capri partly open air and partly covered. This place along with Sheffield Fiesta must rate as one of the plushest gigs I've ever done. To top everything else, the audience were really appreciative of the instrumentals we did before the Fantastics came on. But sadly, this was to be the last gig with Pip.

During this time there was an opportunity to visit Pompeii. Most of the others went but silly me couldn't be bothered to get out of bed. I said I'll do it next time. But unfortunately, I haven't been back to Naples since. Certainly, one of life's regrets!

Jeff Paterson

Our manager was an Australian guy called Jeff Paterson and he and the Fantastics had a big bust up. Possibly because he had them humping gear which was previously unheard of and kept calling them a bunch of Abo's - *or I don't suppose that helped!*

While we were there he went over to the Isle of Capri and dived off a 140 ft cliff into about 6 ft of water and broke just about every bone in his body. After getting plastered up he discharged himself from hospital and we had to take him back to Frankfurt on a stretcher. He was head to foot in plaster and bandages with just holes for his eyes, mouth and nose - a bit like the invisible man, although I doubt many would remember that TV series.

Anyway, he offered us work independently of the Fantastics which we declined. Then sadly for us, Pip decided to go home. Jim, Spam and I agreed to stay on and see what the Fantastics could come up with under a different management.

While we waited, we dragged my Hammond up into the hotel for security. Also staying in our hotel was a band called the Tumbleweeds. Their guitarist was a guy called Roger Dean who'd previously worked with John Mayall (just before Clapton). He was a pretty nifty player and taught me some great chord inversions for 9ths and 13ths etc. which became very useful for me later and even now.

Cannes

Eventually the Fantastics secured a new management contract and gigs were arranged in Cannes and Majorca. But of course, we were short of a lead guitarist. Spam had a friend and previous band mate called Norman who agreed to fly out and join us in France.

So off we went to Cannes which was a long drive. By this time, I was the only one who had any money left as I was saving it to pay my debts, but we had no money for expenses so my money had to be *'borrowed'*. During the long hot drive both the van front sliding doors were kept wide open and I was sat in the left-hand front passenger seat which was offside as it was a right-hand drive, so I got all the dust blown up from the oncoming traffic in my face. At the time I didn't notice any problem, but the following morning I couldn't open my eyes due to conjunctivitis. Fortunately, Spam got me some drops from a pharmacy and I was ok for the first evening's performance.

When we arrived in Cannes it was late evening and we had instructions to go straight to the club to arrange the accommodation etc. There were advertising posters outside the club reading 'Les Fantastique's - Groupe Noir'. The first words out of the club owners' mouth in a terrible panic were, "My God you are not black!" After explaining to her that we were the backing band and the black ones were on the way she calmed down and told us to wait while she arranged for someone to get us something to eat and take us to our hotel. Well, we waited for what seemed hours and to this day I can't remember whether we actually had anything to eat or not but we were eventually taken to our hotel which was on the sea front. I remember asking Jim many years later if we did get anything to eat and he couldn't remember either.

After our first night's performance the woman owner of the club wasn't happy with our normal show and insisted that we did all sorts of stupid medleys instead which we did to pacify her. Beyond that Norman was not a good replacement for Pip, but in fairness to Norman, Pip was one hell of a hard act to follow.

L-R - Spam, Jim and me in Cannes - Photo by Pete Cole

This time was actually the birth of Aquila as Jim and I were that pissed off with how things were going we both decided that we were going to split from the Fantastics and form our own band as soon as we returned to the UK. Putting the gig one side, Cannes was quite a nice place to be, so we made the most of our day times enjoying it.

Can't remember how long we were in Cannes but the next stop was Sloopy's in Palma. Norman moved on to South Africa apparently and we arranged a friend of Jim's called Fred D'Albert from Tony Knight and the Chessmen to fly out to take over on guitar and meet us in Palma.

Fred D'Albert - Photo courtesy of Pete Cole

So, we started the long drive from Cannes to Barcelona where we were to get the ferry across to Majorca. When we arrived in Barcelona the ferry was fully booked forcing us to get a plane with all the gear. Fortunately, the club arranged and paid for this.

The plane that caught fire mid flight

All the previous planes that we travelled on were either Lufthansa or Swissair always scheduled, and all of which were first rate, in a different league to the current UK holiday flights with pathetic leg room.

But Iberian airlines was a world away from Lufthansa and Swissair. This plane looked like a crappy Douglas DC3 with two propeller engines - I know it can't have been as they were allegedly taken out of service ten years previously. But I'd seen better planes in aviation museums.

All our gear including my Hammond went on the luggage travellator and then down a shoot with me nervously watching on. Fortunately for me, my Hammond had a soft landing as it obliterated a pile of suitcases on its descent - clearly many passengers would not have been so happy.

To accommodate all our gear on the plane several seats were removed. Our gear was then strapped in at the back and there were people arguing about seats in Spanish and some people ended up sitting on the floor. 'Health and Safety?' - you must be joking - *no such thing then! Had it been India I guess a few would have been hanging on to the outside too!*

Anyway, it eventually managed to take off, but during the short twenty-minute flight one of the two engines started bellowing black smoke and I could see the propeller stopping then occasionally restarting as the plane wobbled from side to side - *why did I have to be sat that side?*

Mercifully, it landed at Palma airport with a fleet of fire engines chasing it up the runway, to the sound of many screams, just after I'd kissed my ass goodbye. *No doubt they had to do a thorough seat cleaning job on that plane before using it again!*

To top everything else it was also humping it down with rain. Well, they do say that the rain in Spain falls mainly on the *'planes',* so perhaps it's a good idea to keep away from the Spanish airports! Although on this occasion, the rain probably helped put the fire out.

Fortunately, the rain didn't last too long and the club arranged a pickup truck to transport the gear to the club as our van was of course still in Barcelona, although Ragarse did go and fetch it a few days later when the ferries were available again.

The villa from Hell

The accommodation we were given for our stay was an old villa at the top of a hill accessed by a steep dusty track a couple of miles outside Palma. Some taxi drivers refused to go up there as apparently it was built on the site of an ancient satanic temple - *comforting or what?*

There were several bedrooms on both of the two floors with the lounge and shower room downstairs. The two stories were separated by an outside stairway.

It was agreed that the Fantastics would have the downstairs bedrooms and the band would have upstairs and we all shared the downstairs lounge and bathroom etc. Maybe you've seen the film Carry on Abroad where the characters stayed in a half-built hotel called Hells Bells, well this was pretty similar although much older and it didn't *actually* fall down, not then anyway, but only through the grace of God!

Lights would only work occasionally and flicker when they did. Sometimes you got mud and sand out of the taps after the initial electric shock when touching them - apparently the water came from a very unreliable well. I always used to wonder what else might be down there - *maybe the decaying remains of the last guests!*

The electric was 110 volts, I don't know how many amps it was, but apparently, it's the amps that kill you. Getting a shower was seriously dangerous - you had to turn the shower on while your feet were insulated, then get showered without touching any pipework, then get out, dry and insulated again before risking turning it off.

The drainage was obviously a septic tank which was badly in need of emptying as it stank to high heaven. On top of that the windows either didn't close or wouldn't open, the roof leaked when it rained which fortunately was quite rare and the beds were badly in need of replacing. Apart from that it was great, *but best of all it was free!*

After a couple of nights, the rest of the band decided to move out to a nearby hotel they found, but of course they had to pay for that. As I was trying to gather funds to pay off my organ debt which had recently been depleted due to my money being *'borrowed'* for the travelling expenses, I stayed on as did Ragarse, Donald and Marion. The rest of the Fantastics showed up occasionally but were basically here, there, and everywhere. Even though there were plenty of rooms upstairs, Ragarse and I decided to share as the place was positively spooky and of course we chose the best (or least bad) upstairs room.

Sloopy's

Sloopy's was one of the largest disco / clubs in Palma and was a great gig. After we sorted out a few initial voltage problems everything went ok. Fred was an excellent guitarist and fitted in very well. But Jim and I were still determined to part company from the Fantastics as soon as we got home. Everything went well for a few weeks until Juan Carlos the future king of Spain arrived.

For part of the time Jim and I rented a motor scooter and enjoyed buzzing around the island when we weren't working. Thinking back, we were a bit mad - no crash helmets, just shorts and T shirts - no protection at all, driving like lunatics and no travel insurance - *such is youth!*

Ragarse was having an easy time for once as he had no driving to do and no gear to move. Just switch on the organ and amps and that was it. Then he'd just wander round the club. But he had this terrible habit of keeping all his money hanging out of his back pocket. I warned him about this several times. Then one day the inevitable happened, his wad dropped out onto the dance floor. But fortunately, I just happened to see it and grabbed it before anyone else saw it. Did I tell him? No, but I told all the others and hid it in the villa; then gave it back to him the day we went home. I'll never forget the joy on his face. He freely admitted that if he hadn't lost it, he would have just wasted it, so he was overjoyed to have something to take home with him.

Back in the villa

Towards the end of our stay Ragarse spent his time screwing some Swedish chick that he found, presumably in Sloopy's. Every time I went in our room, they were at it - constantly - day and night! The Karma Sutra could have been re-written with what they got up to. This way, that way and every way you could imagine - and probably ways you hadn't even thought possible! So, in order not to feel too lonely or cramp their style, I dragged my mattress downstairs into the living room to be closer to Don and Marion. The downstairs lounge incidentally was a few steps lower than the other downstairs rooms including the bathrooms.

3 in a bed

All was fine for a few nights, then one night I was just getting off to sleep and I saw one of my shoes floating passed my head accompanied by a strange smell. Shit, I knew the place was bloody haunted! I shut my eyes and pretended not to see it. Then Marion got up to go the loo and screamed as she stepped down from their room into the lounge. She didn't scream because she'd seen a ghost as I'd thought, but because she'd stepped into a soggy mess. It turns out that my shoe wasn't floating in mid-air as I'd assumed, it was floating in smelly mirky water. Apparently, the wastewater had backfired up through the shower waste pipe and flooded the lower-level lounge. Gradually it soaked into my mattress and Marion insisted that I retreat to a higher level i.e., their bedroom and as my mattress was wrecked, also insisted that I share their bed for the rest of the night. So, there we were me, Don and Marion all tucked up together! But don't misunderstand me there was absolutely nothing sexual about this. It's amazing how people assume that people who are sleeping in the same bed are doing more than sleeping. Thankfully they never saw what was going on upstairs as it might have given them a few new ideas!

Deported from Spain

Juan Carlos was staying in the hotel next door to Sloopy's and apparently *'he no like a the musica'*, so the police, who he was obviously in cahoots with started making things difficult for us. Initially they brought in a new rule that no-one was allowed to dance to a British band. To enforce this the police were in the club every night making sure that no one moved while we were playing. But apparently the same rule didn't apply to our support act who were a bunch of West Indian lads from Brixton - also British - *pathetic!*

The next crazy event was that Jerry got arrested for apparently getting into a fight with the chief of police's son - obviously this was rigged and Jerry was a very easy target. So, then we could no longer work although it was pretty much close to the end of our stay anyway. Eventually Jerry was released and we were all deported or rather given 24 hours to leave Spain. We all had full page dodgy looking 'Policia' stamps on our passports. I never actually translated what it said in full, but from that point on I didn't return to Spain until I had a new passport several years later.

So, we set off for the long journey back via the ferry to Barcelona and then the long drive through Spain and France to Dieppe to get the Ferry to Newhaven. I've done that same trip numerous times since and it sensibly takes a few days even with motorways. But then there were no motorways and we had to do it without overnight stops with Jim and Ragarse sharing the driving.

Fortunately, we caught the once every 24 hours ferry literally with seconds to spare. I got dropped off first as Blindley Heath was on the A22 between Newhaven and London. So that was the end of the Fantastics for me and Jim, although I did meet them again on several occasions over the next few years.

Aquila

Having returned home Jim and I didn't waste a second moving on. Jim contacted a previous band mate called Phil Childs who was a great bass player. I scoured the Melody Maker ads for a singer / guitarist and found Ralph Denyer.

After numerous phone calls between me Ralph and Jim we hired a practice room in Croydon and we all gelled together perfectly. But something was missing - *George!* We advertised and auditioned a few sax players, but the moment we saw George (Lee), we all knew he was the one without even consulting one another. So, Aquila was born, but initially we again went under the name of Tapestry which was only ever intended to be a temporary name.

Previously Ralph was with a band called Blonde on Blonde the rest of whom were all from Wales. They made two albums and were reasonably successful. Their bass player Richard Hopkins, stayed at Hendon for a while and became a good friend.

Prior to Aquila, George played with numerous pro bands including Ronnie Jones and the Q Set, The Counts and Maxine Brown.

Phil was the oldest member of the band and previously played with numerous bands including Marty Wilde and the Wild Cats.

Hendon

Practice rooms were expensive and we had extremely limited funds. Fortunately, Alistair Crawford the owner of the house at Hendon where Ralph lived allowed us to practice there for free. This became our second home.

Hendon, 1 Denehurst Gardens to be precise was a six-bedroom detached house adjacent to the Hendon Way. Alistair was previously the manager of a paint factory which enabled him to secure the mortgage for the property. To help finance the place he rented out rooms to students and musicians for a generously fair rent and he also cooked an evening meal (usually a big stew or a curry) for all his tenants and anyone else who happened to be visiting. But it wasn't like a landlord / tenant relationship; everyone was friends and really everyone was a winner.

If you've ever seen the 80's TV series 'The Young Ones', it was very much like that. In fact, it wouldn't surprise me if the series was based around Hendon. I remember one episode of the Young Ones when Neil's mother was coming round to visit and everyone was running around like headless chickens trying to clean the place. Well long before the Young Ones, the exact same scenario occurred at Hendon when Alistair's mother was coming to visit. The vacuum cleaner was hunted down and brought back to life. The fridge was turned off to defrost which was probably a good idea anyway as the ice was starting to force the door hinges off. The gearbox from Alistair's car that he was slowly renovating was removed from under the kitchen table. The kitchen sink full of greasy water and used pots that had been there for weeks was dealt with. Windows and surfaces were washed down probably for the first time ever etc., etc.

Then there was the incident with the discovery of a mouse. All sorts of different ways were being considered as to how to evict him, but preferably without killing him. I remember a labyrinth being constructed with a Perspex top, and cheese placed in the centre. The idea being that the mouse would hunt down the cheese and get lost in the maze then collapse with exhaustion. Had this worked it could have been marketed as the ultimate humane mouse trap, but unfortunately it didn't. Clearly even mice are not that stupid! Electrocution was then considered, but this was about as stupid as politely asking the mouse to stick its head in a guillotine. Unfortunately for the mouse it was ultimately eradicated by the normal brutal conventional means.

But believe me Hendon was the place to be. You didn't need to go out for entertainment - it was all there. Musicians used to come from far and wide to visit.

Eventually Alistair even built a recording studio into the lounge which he had soundproofed, with the mixing desk in the large hallway and an insulated viewing window in-between.

Alistair also played in a local semi pro band. I once did a gig with them at their request.

The other locals were always complaining about us as it was a posh Jewish area and from their point of view the house was inhabited by a bunch of undesirables. *But we did genuinely try hard not to upset them!*

Our first trip to Rome

Initially we got a set of material together including several cover version songs and a few instrumentals and managed to get a gig for a month in the Piper Club in Rome. This was towards the end of 1969.

At this point we didn't have a van, but Jim managed to get a small removal van for next to nothing. Initially this had a diesel engine, but he changed it for a petrol one to make it go faster - fortunately Jim was a brilliant mechanic and could solve most problems at the roadside which was very useful. This thing didn't have a heater incidentally, which were optional extras on many vehicles at that time.

So off we went on the 48 hours nonstop journey to Rome via Ostend, Germany and Switzerland. We had no road manager so Jim did most of the driving with a bit of help from Phil. We had a mattress over the cab so that we could take turns at having a kip, although we had a job getting Ralph out of there; when woken he just kept saying, "Are we in Rome yet?"

George was the only band member who didn't smoke and our smoke must have pissed him off something cruel. But occasionally he would bring out a large, fat cigar and choke us all. I'm not sure whether this was his revenge or whether he actually enjoyed them - but of course we all had to grin and bear it! Another thing George always used to do was to shout "Hey!" every time we passed a haystack. I've been irritating my wife doing the same for the last 50 years! Also, during the journey George was reading the Hobbit, so we'd all get regular Bilbo updates.

Well, it got a bit nippy over the Swiss Alps without a heater. I remember we stopped for a meal in Switzerland in a restaurant on top of the Alps just before descending passed Lake Como as we entered Italy - *absolutely breathtaking scenery!* It's amazing how food tastes so much better when you're starving hungry as we all were by then. Apart from brief petrol stops we only had time for that stop and another in Italy somewhere north of Florence. The second stop was at a motorway services where we just got drinks and snacks.

The services was full of *'Topo Gigios'* who was a famous mouse puppet in the 60's. Nearly everything on sale came with a *'free'* puppet. Consequently, everything was grossly expensive as it was all geared into the price. I took one home for my little brother Glyn, - *and apparently only fifty five years later he can't remember what happened to it!*

Thankfully we eventually arrived in Rome safely but all totally knackered, where we met a guy called Luigi who we had to follow to our hotel. Luigi was riding a motor scooter and was a total nutter. I remember we were driving on a six-lane road (three each side) and overtaking in the third lane then the guy in front of Luigi started overtaking into the fourth lane (meant for the oncoming traffic) and then Luigi overtook him into the fifth lane just as the road was splitting into a dual carriageway tunnel. Anyway, through the grace of God Luigi lived long enough to get us to our hotel which was basic but ok. It seemed like every room in the hotel came complete with a complimentary cat which I found most agreeable as I love cats.

Me with my Roman cat!

The Piper Club

Back in the 60's / 70's The Piper club was the largest and most popular night club in Rome. Surprisingly it's still there over sixty years later. Over the years hundreds of British bands have performed there including: The Who, Pink Floyd; The Small Faces and very aptly Colosseum. I feel privileged that our name can be added to the list (twice).

Although it was late autumn, the weather was surprisingly mild but it did rain most nights for about half an hour at the same time each evening, which I thought was very convenient. It was particularly great working there at that time of the year as we got to meet the Roman locals (as against the tourists) who were a great bunch.

The whole point of this gig for us was to have the daytime hours to rehearse and create our own stuff - which we did. By the time we left Rome we'd more or less got enough original material to make an album. And furthermore, we were able to try out our stuff in the evenings with the local audience, mixed in with our non-original material. All went well apart from the fact that the Italians couldn't make chips and like the Germans were incapable of making tea. Sadly, there's not even many establishments left in the UK who can make a decent pot of tea, *I guess it must be a dying art!*

On our last night the band Argent arrived who were taking over from us for the next month. They were there basically for the same reason as us. We enjoyed a chat and a drink with them before packing up all our gear ready for the long drive home in preparation for our next move. We later did a gig with Argent at Exeter University but didn't get a chance to speak with them then and they probably didn't realise that we were the same band as we were Tapestry in Rome then Aquila in Exeter.

The journey home

Now back in those days - long before we joined the EU let alone left it again - going through France with musical instruments was a no-no as you had to have a *'carnet'* - which involved paying a deposit of 50% of the value of the equipment, which all had to be checked and accounted for etc. - as it was all worth much more in France. As we never had that kind of money, our route to Italy was Belgium - Germany - Switzerland - Italy - no problem. Had we known in advance that we were going through France a carnet could have been arranged through a bank - just a guarantee without any money changing hands.

But as winter was setting in, there was no sensible way back over the Alps except through the Mont Blanc Tunnel into France! So, we thought we'd risk it. As told previously Jim and I had worked in France with The Fantastics earlier in the year and got in from Germany without a carnet and also from Spain on our return, so we thought maybe they wouldn't notice that we were English - *as if!*

As we had to return through France, our agent arranged us some gigs in Paris on the way back, and we had instructions to meet M. Jean Bernard in a café in Paris about 36 hours after leaving Rome.

24 hours stranded in the Alps with no heater

When we arrived at the opening of the Monte Blanc Tunnel after having left the Italian border, unsurprisingly we were stopped for the carnet. The money that we all made in Rome was nowhere near enough, so we hung around for a bit and tried negotiating, which was quite difficult as we didn't speak French and they didn't speak English. Also, by this time, it was freezing cold and belting it down with snow. Our next line of action was to go back into Italy to see if we could find an alternative route, like a smaller, more difficult crossing into Switzerland. Jim could do it; *he could do anything!* But at the Italian border they decided that they also wanted a carnet; normally the Italians didn't bother about such things. So, we were stuck in no man's land between the two borders, and it was getting colder and the snow was getting deeper - and of course we had no heater. I didn't think it was possible to be so cold and still alive! But we managed to refrain from huddling up to one another to share body warmth - *that would have been a step too far!*

Then we tried phoning the British consulate in Turin. They weren't much use; they just told us to dump the gear on top of the mountain and go home without it. My organ cost me a bloody fortune and I hadn't even half-paid for it, so that wasn't an option. Even if the others had decided to do that - which they didn't even consider - I would have stayed there and died with my organ!

By then, night had turned back into day and it was getting even colder - if that was possible. Ralph had a sleeping bag which we shared - one at a time - to keep the blood from freezing!

The customs men had three eight-hour shifts and we tried each one in turn to see if one was more understanding of our plight - but they weren't. Each shift was as miserable as the last! It was 1969, only 25 years after we won the bloody war; you'd think that they might have been at least a little compassionate! Phil - who could speak a little French - tried pleading with them on the grounds that we all had mothers worrying about us, but his French wasn't that good; he was probably accidentally calling them a bunch of mother fuckers! *He might as well have been for the good it did!*

Anyway, after we'd tried all the shifts and it was night again, we thought that, as we'd been there that long, that they'd hardly notice us if we coasted into the tunnel quietly with the engine switched off. Worth a try, as it was downhill and the barrier was open! Well, we got about 25 metres and they started firing warning shots at us. At least I think they were warning shots, but we thought we'd better stop and see what happens next. One of the bullets went through the top rear of the van - *street cred or what?*

Well, we got a heavy on-the-spot fine for that but, surprisingly, they then arranged us a carnet for a reduced deposit, which was still a substantial amount, and was more or less every penny we had (barring expenses) to continue.

Free at last

At last, we were free and we'd got into France. I'll never forget the first village the other side of the tunnel called Les Houches. The place had a really magical and inviting look about it. We stopped there in the snow at a little skiing hotel decorated with fairy lights which was still open at about 3:00 am where we had jambon sandwiches and black coffee. I don't even drink coffee - especially black - but I remember that tasting better than anything before or since, as I was that cold and hungry. And we got such a warm welcome there, just after I was cursing every Frenchman in existence and swearing I'd never set foot in the place ever again.

Then we plodded on. After descending the Alps and we left the snow behind it was then raining and foggy. At that time, they were constructing the main motorway from Lyon to Paris, so it was also mud and road works all the way. But the fog was holding us up more. I remember one of the lads saying, "Jesus Christ where did this fucking fog come from?" and I said to myself, "It would be much better if you asked him to lift it and perhaps a little more politely". Then miraculously the fog lifted but only in a tunnel in front of us for the rest of the journey.

Shortly we saw some lights and stopped at what we thought was a cafe, which turned out to be a workman's hut, but they kindly gave us all a free coffee (black of course) and a bit of a warmup in their hut to help us on our way. *What a difference between normal people and bureaucrats!*

Not long before reaching Paris we came to a Jimburger which was the French equivalent of Wimpy where we all got fed and watered.

Nightmare in Paris

Next stop: Paris. But we were over 24 hours late. We thought we'd go to the cafe just in case Jean Bernard was still there. Well, he was. And very disgruntled. He just got in the van and said, "I av zee gig, you are not ere - vot can I do? Fuck zem, you know. Zis vay, zis vay." - *French accent and lots of Gaelic shrugs.*

We said, "Have we got a gig or not?"

"I av zee gig, you are not ere vot can I do? Fuck zem, you know. Zis vay, zis vay." - *More Gaelic shrugs.*

"For you, I av zee competition. If you win, you get paid. If you don't - *big Gaelic shrug!* Fuck zem, you know. Zis way, zis way," - continuing to give directions to goodness knows where.

"Listen", we said. "We're not working for nothing - we're professionals!"

To which the reply was, "Don't vorry, don't vorry. I am zee judge. Fuck zem, you know. Zis vay!"

We finally arrived at some crappy little French club which was about three floors up. So, we all walked up the stairs to see if it was worth getting the gear out.

"You bloody Engleesh, you all ze same. You av all zis gear and you valk up all zees stairs and you CARRY NOTHING!" stamping his feet as he got the last words out.

"Listen man, give us a break. We haven't slept or eaten for three days!"

"But I av not slept for twenty years!" - *Big Gaelic shrug!* Apparently, he was an insomniac and never slept - probably all that French black coffee!

"And if you have not eaten how come you ave ze Jimburger matches?"

Clearly, he was also a bit of a sleuth!

We eventually dragged all the gear up the stairs and won the competition (unsurprisingly). But our winnings were about half of what we should have got paid anyway, and the hotel was supposed to be paid, but it wasn't - *big rip-off!* And by today's standards, health and safety would certainly have closed the hotel down ten times over! The hotel room for all of us consisted of two double beds and one single. I can't remember who got the single I think we drew straws but I remember waking up next to George and thank God that he wasn't dreaming about his wife.

We were assured that things were going to get better; although we weren't convinced, we decided to continue anyway. The next gig was in a plush château. I think it was a four-year-old kid's birthday party, and he'd been put to bed so that everyone else could get pissed on his behalf. Well, the gig went fine, but again we didn't get paid the previously agreed amount.

Ali Baba's Cave

At the end of the gig Phil and I noticed a small but very hot storage heater in one of the back rooms, and we decided to *'borrow'* it to try and warm the van up a bit. So, we unplugged it, chucked a speaker cover over it, and struggled out with it unnoticed - bloody heavy, as it was full of bricks! When we got it to the van, we found that the others had been *'borrowing'* loads of silver; don't judge us, we were starving musicians who'd just been ripped off! I'm not sure who nicked what, but the stuff was everywhere; it was like Ali Baba's cave in there!

But then Jean Bernard decided he wanted a lift back into Paris, so we hurriedly chucked all the booty onto the mattress above - the heater included - but it caught fire. Jim was driving, with Jean Bernard sat next to him saying, "Vot is zat smell?" - while the rest of us were beating the flames out!

It was a relief when Jean Bernard got out. Then we managed to get things back to normal or as normal as possible in the back of the van. The next night we did the last less-eventful French gig, but then we realised that we had to have the van checked at the customs to get our carnet money back and we'd got all this *'loot'*. Unfortunately, we decided that it had to go, so we dumped it in someone's dustbin after the gig, on the way back to the port. I think Ralph cunningly saved one silver ashtray that he hid in his undies. I have a vague memory of a little old lady giving us the thumbs up from her bedroom window as we were sticking the rest of the stuff in her bin, but I'm not sure whether I dreamt that or not.

At the port we did fortunately get most of our carnet money back. Jim commented later that the look on the custom guy's face was priceless when he saw how much they had to give us, and they had to raid a cash machine to get enough money for us - I must have been asleep then.

Having returned to the UK we continued getting our original stuff together in preparation for making an LP (vinyl of course in those days). Our next step was to agree on a name for the band and secure a record contract. We almost chose the name 'Animal Farm', then when some recording agent came to see us from the US, he said our material wasn't fitting with the name. Then went on to sing his interpretation of what he thought we should be doing which went, "Animal Farm, Animal Farm, we're all living on Animal Farm", accompanied by an idiotic little dance. Well, that put an instant end to that name completely *and the agent!* And

George amused us regularly with his rendition of the stupid agent's song.

By then 1969 was drawing to a close. We were offered more work in France with M. Bernard but unsurprisingly we declined.

Lulu's party

Our last gig of the year was a private New Year's Eve party for Lulu at a Chinese Restaurant somewhere in the West End. Obviously, there was a lot of influential people there. It was a fabulous night and after our set, we all sat down for a Chinese meal with everyone else. I didn't see Lulu by the way, but I didn't look for her either, but I guess she must have been there somewhere!

At some point during the party, I got champagne squirted all over my face, by George I think, which I wiped off with some crepe paper that was knocking about. When I looked in a mirror in the morning, I was shocked to see that my face was multicoloured - orange, blue, red, and green. I didn't make it home that night but spent the night at Phil's in Notting Hill; I'm not even quite sure how we got there.

As a result of this gig a film producer who was there asked us to record a short piece of music for the actress Carol White to do a striptease to on a film called 'The Man Who Had Power Over Women'. This was all done and dusted the following week. To this day I haven't seen the film, but apparently it wasn't a great success.

Signed to RCA

Not long after this Jim and a couple of other guys at Hendon came up with the name Aquila which we all immediately agreed to.

We then began negotiations with a few companies for a record deal and eventually secured one that gave us a good unreturnable advance royalty payment with RCA via Lew Futterman in the US. We were assigned a producer called Patrick Campbell-Lyons who was a former member of the 60's UK group 'Nirvana'.

Aquila's album cover by Keith Besford

Within a few weeks contracts were signed (although they did *try* to swap pounds for dollars which they said was a *'slip of the pen'*) and we began recording. We used a recording studio on the Old Kent Road owned by Manfred Mann which was 8 track, but had one of the first 16 track mixing decks.

The design for the cover was assigned to a friend called Keith Besford who at the time was an art student / musician living at Hendon. I'm glad to say that I am still in touch with Keith who now lives in Northumbria where he came from. The *'eagle'* on the cover incidentally was a drawing of *'Goldie'* the golden eagle who then resided at London Zoo.

We originally wanted to get an eagle's cry at the beginning of the album. So, Ralph took some recording equipment to London Zoo and asked the keeper if he could record Goldie. The keeper said, "Yeh, you can if you want mate, but I've been here thirty years and haven't heard him make a sound yet!" So, we gave up on that one, then briefly tried recording a crow instead, but eventually gave up on that too.

I can't remember the exact date the album was released but little time was lost between mastering and releasing. In retrospect there were many things I and no doubt the others too would have done differently on the album, although I guess that's the same with everything. But overall, we were all fairly satisfied and we had a unique distinctive sound helped on by the harmonic riffs that George and I created. Kid Jenson on Radio Luxembourg gave us a great deal of promotion which we were of course grateful for, but RCA generally were not good and in retrospect perhaps it was a mistake signing with them.

Aquila L-R Phil, Ralph, George, me & Jim

We did several UK gigs including the Country Club, West Hampstead both on our own and with Elton John, The Fickle-Pickle Club, Southend with David Bowie, The Roundhouse, the Plumpton Festival, Southampton Uni, Leeds Uni, plus many more.

Some of the bands we worked with included:

- Free

- Argent

- Atomic Rooster

- If

- Colosseum

- Mathews Southern Comfort

- Groundhogs

- Procol Harum

- Elton John

- Genesis

- David Bowie

- Juicy Lucy

- Vander Graff Generator

- Plus, loads more at the Plumpton Festival

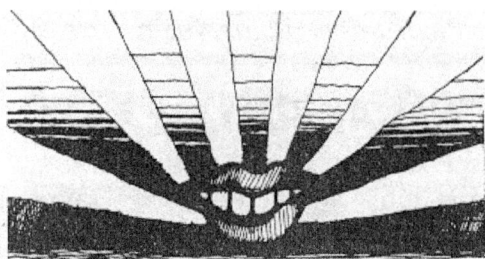

IF · AQUILA · GENESIS · JULIANS TREATMENT
6·30 – 11p.m. Friday 3rd July, 1970
College for the Distributive Trades, 107 Charing Cross Rd, WC2.
Tickets 6/- in advance from Steve Franklin C.D.T,
30 Leicester Sq. London WC2.
S.A.E. and Postal Order please. 10/- at door.

The gigs with Bowie, Elton John, and Genesis

When we worked with David Bowie at the Fickle - Pickle Club, it was ironic but Bowie was supporting us! And this was about the same time as his original 'Space Oddity' hit record. But at the time he certainly wasn't the icon that he later became. Thinking of him now, you'd imagine him to arrive at gigs with a juggernaut full of gear and a stack of roadies, which I'm sure was the reality later. But back then it was nothing like that. He arrived in a Transit sized Bedford van and he and the band lugged all their own gear in. As we had the stage they had to set up in the smaller room on the floor!

When we worked with Elton John at the Country Club it was just after his first number one album, so even then he was immensely popular. The Country Club was a fantastic venue which regularly hosted huge acts. But it was also a brilliant environment where the audience could get right up to the very low stage. In fact, when Elton was on, I was stood virtually next to him having a good look at what he was doing. *He even winked at me; heaven forbid!*

After our set apparently Ralph had a good conversation with Elton who was very complimentary of our band.

The gig with Genesis was the same day as the Elton John gig, so it was a bit of a rush to get there and I never even caught a glimpse of them or heard them, but again it was very early days for them! 'If' was the main act on that occasion - *a brilliant band who are now sadly forgotten!*

Cigarette coupons

Back in those days there used to be coupons in cigarette packets that you could save and redeem for various things. Curiously George, the only one who didn't smoke used to collect them. We all gave him ours and he also used to go around the clubs at the end of the evenings checking the discarded packets which were everywhere. One day he picked up an empty packet to check it then threw it down again in disappointment and some guy came up to him offering him a cigarette and said, "Here you go mate, have one of mine". *Kindness is everywhere!*

Aquila L-R Jim, me (top), Phil, Ralph & George

If you're wondering why we all look so miserable in the photos, it's because it was uncool to smile in those days and we were also perpetually skint! But they were the best of times - *and we were all smiling on the inside!*

Rome again

By late July we were off to Rome again but this time as Aquila doing our own material. By then we had a Transit which was faster and more comfortable than the removal van. But it was still a long way. We were booked for the whole of August. I remember this as my 21st birthday 30th July was spent travelling for the whole 24 hours and more. My mother made me a big, iced fruit cake which we shared out during the journey. Also with us on this trip was Jim's wife Myja and George's lovely wife Sherifa.

We still went via Belgium, Germany and Switzerland to avoid the French carnet, but this journey was much more comfortable as it was summer and we had a heater which we only needed at night and over the Alps. We stopped again at the same Swiss restaurant on top of the Alps, but instead of taking the central route through Italy, this time we took the coast road through Pisa to have a look at the famous *'tower'*. Well, it really does lean! We stopped there for a short while to take a few photos. Apparently, you can normally go up the tower, but when we were there, it wasn't possible due to stability renovations. Every time I think of this place it reminds me of Russ Abbott's hilarious sketch of the rooftop restaurant in the leaning tower!

Later as we arrived in Rome there was a big Aquila poster by the Piper club which made us feel very proud. We stayed at the same hotel as before but thankfully didn't need Luigi's help to find it this time. My favourite cat was still there and appeared pleased to see me, *but in reality, probably didn't give a shit!*

Me at the Colosseum

Well Rome seemed so much better in the summer and we took advantage of the sunshine to see all the sites, but it was incredibly hot. There was no air con then; to keep cool I used to sit in the shower on cold for about twenty minutes a few times a day. But the dodgiest thing was crossing the roads with the crazy Italian drivers. I don't think they were singling us out in particularly but it did seem that way. And clearly pedestrians didn't have any priority on zebra crossings. Maybe you got a reduced priced funeral and a free *'Topo Gigio'* if you got flattened on one! *Crossing the road by the Colosseum was virtually suicidal!*

After the gig we sometimes went to St Peter's Square in the early hours of the morning which was a serene experience. But they wouldn't allow me into the Vatican (in the daytime) as I'd got long hair and was wearing sandals, so I guess that would have ruled out Jesus too! - *Bloody idiots!*

Although Rome is inland, the nearest seaside at Ostia is only about a 25 minutes' drive, so we occasionally went there to enjoy a bit of sea breeze. Jim also tried unsuccessfully to teach me to swim, but I did eventually learn later.

In the early evenings we'd eat out in various open air *'piazza'* restaurants a truly magical experience and no doubt romantic for couples. Most had a fountain in the centre and all sorts of potted plants scattered around as well as serenading musicians. If you could recreate the ambience of these places and bring it to the UK you'd make a fortune. *But they still couldn't make sodding tea!*

Ralph gets pissed

During this time, I collected some miniature wine bottles (with wine) which were purchased for approx. 50 lire each (next to nothing). Knowing that I hardly drink Ralph was curious as to why I did this, to which I replied, "I just like the bottles". - "So, you don't really want the wine then?" - "No not really, I just want the *bottles!" Perhaps I shouldn't have said this!*

Each bottle contained 100ml of wine and there were over twenty which equated to more than two litres. I'm told that mixing wine is not a good idea. And in this collection, there was a good variety of reds, whites, and rosés, all from different grapes and all with nice bottles.

Anyway, one afternoon unbeknown to everyone else Ralph decided to have a solo wine tasting extravaganza and drank the lot - which made him totally paralytic. And we'd got to go on stage with him in that state. Well, we dragged him to the club, sat him on the stage with his guitar and did what we could - mainly instrumentals. After the gig he was puking everywhere and we couldn't get him out of the van where he stayed all night. Early the following morning before he was baked to a crisp in the van, we managed to get him back into the hotel and into bed. I asked him if I could get him anything and he just said, "Ice!" So, I went out and found a watermelon man and had a hard job explaining to him that no I didn't want a slice of watermelon or a whole one, I just wanted the block of ice that the slices of melons were standing on. Eventually I managed to buy some. Fortunately, after a day in bed with my block of ice which eventually soaked his bed through, he recovered enough to work normally again.

Baring that slight hiccup the gig went really well. Then we had to undertake the long return journey. As it was still summer there was no worries about getting stuck in the Alps and being forced to return through France. So, what could possibly go wrong?

The journey home

Well not long into the journey the clutch developed a fault in the hydraulic system preventing the clutch from disengaging. For anyone who doesn't know what this means, it means that whether the clutch pedal was up or down it performed as though it was up, making moving off, changing gear and stopping extremely difficult. And we'd got to travel over a thousand miles. Taking out breakdown cover or travel insurance never even entered our heads.

Anyway, it can be done with difficulty. Moving off involved switching the engine off, moving the gear lever into first gear, then turning the ignition key allowing the vehicle to jump forwards until it got going in first gear which was only easily possible downhill or level - had we stopped on a steep uphill road we would have been stuffed. Changing gear can then be achieved by getting the revs just right and tapping the gear lever into the appropriate gear. To stop was easy, by just tapping the gear lever into neutral, braking and coasting to a halt. But the most difficult by far was moving off, especially in traffic and virtually impossible uphill. Well Jim managed to do this for the whole journey back and also managed to manoeuvre it on and off the ferry which was extremely tricky. It is something I could do now after years of experience, but I certainly couldn't have done it then. *Good old Jim!*

We had planned on stopping at Radio Luxembourg on the way home for an interview with Kid Jensen, but unfortunately due to the clutch problem we would have arrived too late, so we had to give that a miss - *shame!*

Having returned home, the clutch problem was simple to fix. I can't remember whether it was the master cylinder or the slave cylinder rubbers, but either way it was an easy fix with the parts being readily available in London.

Apparently both Rome and Sheffield are built on seven hills and very occasionally I really can see the resemblance in Sheffield, mainly when looking through arched alleyways on the top of the hills - it's taken me by surprise a few times.

Despite chucking money in the Trevi fountain I never returned to Rome again, although I have travelled extensively for which I am truly grateful.

The Paradiso Amsterdam

We did more gigs in England before our next little adventure which was Germany and Holland. Again, travelling Dover - Ostend, we did a couple of gigs in Germany (can't remember where) then on to the Exit Club in Rotterdam which was the sister club of the Paradiso. After the Exit Club a couple of the staff there kindly put us up for the night in their flat on put-you-up beds. Then onto the infamous Paradiso in Amsterdam.

This joint was most certainly a den of iniquity - *joint being the appropriate word!* Saint or sinner you could not be in that place without being stoned unless you stopped breathing. Dope was literally everywhere. Even at the bar people were openly rolling joints. Many people were laid out on the floor gazing up at the ceiling where they were showing Tom and Jerry cartoons.

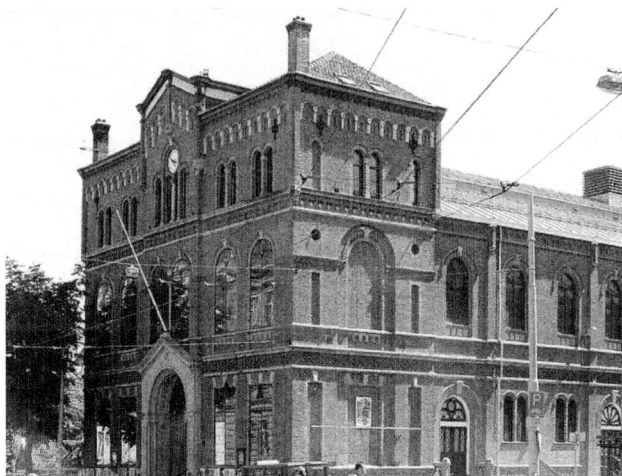

The Paradiso Amsterdam

In terms of a London comparison, I would say that the Roundhouse at Chalk Farm is the most similar, although the Paradiso is not round, and is probably higher with a two-storey gallery around the periphery. *Both were magic venues!*

While we were playing there was little audience response and I initially thought we were going down like a lead balloon. Then some guy stumbled onto the stage with a joint and said, "We think you're really great man, just can't get it together to clap!"

Even in the office when we went to collect our earnings at the end of the evening the staff were smoking joints.

We were then given directions to the hotel which they'd assigned for us. Even the guy on reception there was smoking a joint. Anyway, we had all our money in a small wooden box. I suggested that we share it all out in the morning, but the others insisted that we sort it then, which we did, leaving the expenses in the box. As it happened that turned out to be a very good idea.

Well, sometime during the night all our rooms were broken into and we were robbed. The cash box with the expenses went and sadly also George's money, but fortunately no one else's. It certainly left a bad taste in our mouths about Amsterdam. But overall, I love the Dutch people, just not the one who robbed us! And I also love Dutch apple pie - *and the cheese!*

When I meet Dutch people now and mention that I've played at the Paradiso I'm immediately exalted to a higher level! One of them asked the wife if she used to be a groupie - *he's probably still recovering from his injuries!*

The end of Aquila

After returning from Amsterdam, we did a few more gigs in the UK, then there was some sort of argument between our management and agency resulting in the gigs stopping and it all grinded to a halt.

I more than anyone (I think) wanted to resurrect Aquila and this was my intention for some time to come. But in the meantime, we all had to find other sources of income.

Geno Washington

As mentioned previously Geno Washington and the Ram Jam Band was originally formed by guitarist / producer Pete Gage who later formed Elkie Brook's band and wrote several of her songs. During the lifetime of Geno's band, it was *'inhabited'* by numerous musicians, as were similar bands at the time such as Carl Douglas, Jimmy James, The Fantastics, the Flirtations etc.

A little later Jim joined Geno Washington and the Ram Jam Band and very shortly after I did too, but I only ever saw this as a stop gap as it was still my intention to resurrect Aquila. Their guitarist at that time was Alan Griffin who I mentioned earlier (The Subjects) and their bass player was Roger Flavell. Tony Hall was one of the sax players and Brent Scott Carter was the other one - all great musicians.

During this time the band decided that they were going to branch out on their own with some original material. We had brief get together and I'm sure it would have been good, but my heart was still with Aquila, so being honest and not wanting to waste their time, I told them that I wasn't interested. Shortly afterwards my services were no longer required!

Apparently, very shortly after my departure the group disbanded and went their separate ways.

A Time of Reflection

Over the last couple of years my Hammond had taken a fair battering and was desperately in need of some serious attention externally and internally. So, I decided to take some time out to get it renovated. My elder brother Steve, who was an electronics engineer, recovered it externally with wood Formica and also sorted out the inside. My father then made me two strong boxes for it so that it wouldn't get damaged anymore in transit.

Me, Steve and my renovated Hammond

During this time, I got a temporary job driving a taxi in Redhill working for a great guy called Wally Belton who treated me like one of his sons. After not too long he sold me a car and gave me a Hackney Carriage plate free which at that time used to changed hands for over £1000.

I also passed my advanced driving test, again with the help of my father who was in fact the eighth person to pass it many years previously. This proved to be very useful to me later.

And low and behold my debts were paid which came as a joyful surprise to me as I never kept an account of them at all. - I just considered it to be a never-ending cloud of doom!

At this time, I also decided to pursue the Fantastics for what they owed me which I did have a detailed account of. Between Jim and I we had a solicitor send them a letter and although they weren't overjoyed about it, they paid us everything that we were owed. They'd got a saying going at the time - 'TCB' (take care of business), well that's what I was doing - taking care of my business!

André Previn

Once while driving my taxi, I picked up a pleasant American chap who got in the front of the car with me. He wanted to go to his home in Reigate but also pick some stuff up from a car that he'd had to abandon the night before in a flood.

On the way we were chatting about all sorts and nothing, then when we got to the abandoned car the road was still flooded. He said he wouldn't blame me if I didn't want to attempt getting through it and we could take a long way round if necessary. But I got through it ok. Then he went to the abandoned car and picked up a pile of music manuscripts. I said, "Oh music, I'm a musician I play in a pop group, what do you do?" to which he replied very modestly, "Oh I conduct the London Symphony Orchestra!"....... Shit! ...... Well, I'd heard the name André Previn but had no idea what he looked like, and I thought he would have been French with a name like that.

This was not long before his famous appearance on the Morecambe and Wise show when Eric Morecambe played the piano very badly and asked André what was wrong and he said, "Well you were playing all the wrong notes!" Then Eric grabbed hold of him by the lapels and said, "I was playing all the right notes, - but not necessarily in the right order!"

The crazy thing is that André Previn was probably more well known for that short sketch than his whole time with the LSO. But he was a genuinely nice man and was probably quite refreshed to speak to someone who didn't know who he was - *well, maybe!*

Tommy Hunt

My organ was eventually all in perfect working order and looking great, but I hadn't even considered what I was going to do next. Then Roger Flavell the bass player from Geno phoned me out of the blue and asked me if I wanted to join the Tommy Hunt band with him. At first, I was a bit reluctant as it didn't sound up my street, but I agreed to give it a go. It actually turned out to be very much up my street.

Tommy Hunt was a US soul singer. Before going solo in the late 60's he was with a popular US group called the Flamingoes. I believe he started working in the UK in about 1969, apparently Ronnie the bass player with the Fantastics had worked with him previously, which I didn't know until our reunion fifty years later.

The other band members were Kevan Forgarty on guitar who was first class - as good as Pip, but very different! I can't remember the name of the drummer who was with us when I joined, but he was very shortly replaced by Tex Marsh who was excellent, and of course Roger on bass who was also excellent. I'm truly privileged to have played with such a fantastic bunch of musicians.

At the time they were working in Rotherham, so they sent Ron the road manager down to Blindley Heath to collect me and my gear. I had a chance to hear them for one night in Rotherham with Chris Holmes the guy I was replacing. I remember having a great chat with Chris and it turned out that he also had had an encounter with M. Jean Bernard in France. Many years later I conversed with Chris a great deal via the internet, he was very complimentary about my playing as I was of his. He was a genuinely lovely man but has sadly now passed on.

L-R Roger, me, Tommy, (Unknown drummer) & Kevan

I took over from Chris on the next night which was in Liverpool. After a few weeks I settled into the band comfortably. You could always see where Chris had been previously as he left a trail of destruction behind him in the form of burnt chair arms where he missed the ashtray due to his bad eyesight.

Kevan had previously worked with Timebox (with Chris), who had a residency at the Marquee club and also the Dave Divani 4.

Tex had worked with numerous successful bands including the Quiet 5, Melody Fair, J.J. Jackson, Simon K & the Meantimers and more.

Roger worked with The Magic Roundabout, The Bandwagon, Grand Union and of course Geno where we met. I guess fifty plus years on these names mean nothing to most people, but they were well known bands in their days.

Life gets easy

Compared to what I'd done previously this was a doddle, as we were doing cabaret for seven nights in each place - mainly up North. And for once I was earning good money and all my debts were paid. We always stayed in decent guest houses on a full board basis. I mostly shared rooms with Tex and we'd re-enact Tony Hancock's 'Blood Donor' script virtually word for word on a daily basis - Why? - God knows - *but I so miss Tex!* When working in the Northwest we all stayed at Kevin's mother's house in Southport which was even better.

So, life was easy, only working about an hour and a half each night, time to kill in the daytime, money to spare and no gear to shift. No wonder we were all into having jokes on one another. The most common one was exploding cigarettes. These were tiny exploding capsules added to the cigarettes and usually exploded as soon as lit. But we all got quite adept at this and could push the capsules deep into the cigarettes unnoticed so that they exploded when least expected. Consequently, when being given a cigarette, they were accepted with great suspicion and always inspected very closely. One of my greatest successes at this was at the Wookey Hollow club in Liverpool when I gave one to Ron the roadie and it exploded with a big blue flash at the precise moment he connected the mains cable. I can still see his face now, peering out from behind a pile of speakers - *priceless!*

Kevan, Tex and Roger were all into golf which is how they spent much of their daytime hours. I just used to wander around whatever town we happened to be in.

In the late evenings when we'd finished working there were no wild drug filled parties, far from it, I used to enjoy thrashing Kevan at chess over a cup of tea, or sometimes we'd all play cards so that Kevan could get his own back. I was pretty good at chess and once had a game with Ben E. King in the dressing room at the Revolution club, London, but on that occasion, it was me who got thrashed!

When working in or near Derby we regularly stayed at a guest house called 'Paul's' run by a couple of gays. They were great in the fact that they would cater for our needs - *no, absolutely not like that!* Like, at most guest houses if you didn't get up for breakfast by a certain time you'd miss it, but they realised that we worked late so if we wanted breakfast at 1:00 pm it was no problem etc., and if we wanted a cup of tea and a slice of toast at 3:00 am we could help ourselves.

One time when we stayed there, we asked them if there were any descent pubs in the area that we could go to before our show. One of them gave us detailed directions to a place the other side of town which turned out to be a bloody gay bar. When we next saw him, he said in his camp voice, "Well you did ask me, I can only give you my opinion - what did you expect?" *Well, you've got to laugh!*

Just down the road from Paul's was a great joke shop which we all used to frequent individually so that the others didn't see what we were buying. *One time I sneaked off there and found Roger inside!*

We played at all the top cabaret clubs throughout the UK such as:

- Wakefield theatre club
- Showboat Middlesbrough
- Sheffield Fiesta
- Kingsway Casino Southport
- Baileys Cavendish clubs nationwide
- Mecca circuit nationwide
- Caesars Palace London

- Double Diamond Caerphilly

- And many, many more great venues

But these were totally different to the gigs I did with Aquila and perhaps bordering on what I did with the Fantastics. To be honest I liked all of them.

Many of the cabaret clubs at that time had a casino attached. I don't know why but I really like the casino environment even though I hate gambling. I learnt my lesson about gambling many years earlier when I lost half a crown (12.5p) to a one arm bandit on Brighton pier.

Free shirts

Whilst working in Wakefield, we were offered free stage shirts from the Double TWO shirt factory as a promotional event for them. This was back in the days when clothes were actually made in Britain rather than some sweat shop in China or wherever.

We had to go to the factory to collect them, be photographed wearing the shirts and be interviewed by the local press. But Kevan couldn't be bothered to go for some reason so he sent Ron the roadie in his place (pretending to be him) with strict instructions that he was collar size 17". It was quite farcical as we had to keep correcting Ron on several of the questions asked by the press, like how to spell his name etc. And of course, the shirt didn't fit him properly. Anyway, we got the free shirts (two each) and used them on stage regularly. I always laugh when I pass a Double TWO outlet.

There were sometimes other freebies that musicians could get, but they all came with conditions. The drummer before Tex used a complimentary Premier drum kit with the condition that he used it on all performances. When Tex replaced him there was an incredible difference apart from the fact that Tex was much better, the sound of Tex's Ludwig kit was *far* superior to the Premier kit - *so clearly some freebies are not worth having!*

Support acts

Mainly with Tommy we were topping the bill and had a couple of support acts. The only time I remember that we weren't topping was when we supported Ken Dodd who was brilliant, but he wouldn't get off stage - *his act was over three hours!*

One of our support acts was Cannon and Ball in their early days. During their act Tommy (Cannon) told Bobby that he didn't need him anymore and to pack his stuff and go home, resulting in Bobby walking through the audience with his tatty suitcase in tears. All the audience thought it was for real and Tommy practically got lynched - *so funny!* We were doubling that week between Barnsley and Doncaster, and we always arrived at the second club during that part of their act.

Another regular support act was a clown called Windy Blow. He used to blow balloons up and twist them into various animal shapes. But off stage he was just like the

Simpsons 'Crusty the Clown' when *he* was off stage. He used to stay at our hotel so I regularly had breakfast with him. His offstage manner used to amuse me far more than his act. Can you imagine what it would be like to have breakfast with chain smoking Crusty the Clown? Crusty could have been modelled around this guy! But most of the support acts I never even saw.

My new speaker

With my newfound wealth I decided to have a powerful rotary speaker custom made for me by a guy in London called Bill Dunne. He used to make them for several big groups at the time so came highly recommended. When it was ready, Ron the roadie drove me and my organ down to London to have it all wired up. On the way back I stopped at Hendon to see Ralph and had a great jam with drummer Jim Tooney who also lived there. At the time Jim Tooney was playing with Titus Groan, but later played for Annie Lennox.

Anyway, after initially using my new speaker with the band I discovered that it needed more treble - couldn't make the Hammond scream enough. So, I phoned Bill Dunne who said there was no problem and he could fix it for me, but of course I had to take it back to London.

At this time, we were working in Sheffield so I decided to drive down on my own overnight in the van, get it sorted first thing in the morning then drive back to Sheffield -

missing a night's sleep - no problem at my age then. At the time we were staying in Wakefield and by the time I'd got my gear back on stage in Sheffield, had I driven back up to Wakefield I would have had to drive straight back to Sheffield, so I stayed put in the club and met Janet who was waitressing there. I talked her into making me a cup of tea and got chatting with her.

As we were working in the North almost constantly, I saw a lot of Janet and we became an item (and later married). I remember our first date was at the launderette in Nether Edge Sheffield! During our married life of over fifty years, we've only ever had one argument - *the only trouble is, it started fifty years ago!*

Tommy goes to Australia

Curiously Tommy's manager was Jeff Paterson the Australian guy who previously managed the Fantastics who we transported from Naples to Frankfurt on a stretcher. He arranged a month's tour of Oz for Tommy, but he could only take Kevan and possibly Tex with him. In fact, there was great uncertainty as to whether Tex was going or not. Anyway, Roger, Tex and I started getting some material together to work on our own - and it was going *very* well. We got some fantastic instrumentals going - some great Booker T stuff and others.

Also, at this time one night the Fantastics turned up at one of our gigs. They were looking for another band and heard about us. It was good to see them again. I thought they might be a bit miffed about me previously *'taking care of my business'* but they weren't or at least they didn't seem to be. Don, Marion and I were reminiscing about the Spanish Villa, our night in bed together and other previous events.

Well, they tried to negotiate our band away from Tommy. I told them to see Kevan. But the bottom line was that they couldn't afford us! I guess part of the problem was that with there being four of them, there was simply too many people to pay!

At the last minute it was agreed that Tex was to go with Kevan and Tommy to Australia, so that put pay to what Tex, Roger and I had been getting together.

For a short while I went home then moved in with Janet in Sheffield. Unbeknown to me then, Tex *didn't* go to Australia and he and Roger were looking for me to resume what we'd started and had even got some gigs lined up. This was my greatest missed opportunity as both Roger and Tex were superb and they brought out the very best in me! When I was doing an improvised solo, I only had to make a very slight hint and they were both there with me putting all the accents bang in the right place. It was like we were one mind! *An incredible experience!*

Kings Swing

I then decided to stay in Sheffield and answered an advert for a local group called King's Swing who were looking for an organist. I did pretty much to them what Pip did to Tapestry - *I blew them away!* They couldn't believe their luck having me join them. The lineup was just organ, bass, drums and vocals. It turned out to be a good little band and we got lots of local gigs, and never ventured out of Yorkshire / Derbyshire which suited me fine. We became very popular around the area and although the gigs were increasing week by week, I took a part time temporary job doing road censuses in the late afternoons and sometimes early mornings.

Meanwhile Tommy and Kevan had returned from Australia and were back working in the UK again. Unfortunately for us, Roger had found work elsewhere, so the only original band members were Kevan and Tex who came looking for me. Remember there were no mobile phones then and Janet didn't even have a landline.

Back with Tommy

They eventually found me and I initially declined the offer to return to them, saying I didn't want to leave Sheffield. But the pressure was on. Tommy agreed to hire me a car so that I could return to Sheffield every night, so I eventually agreed although I insisted on honouring the final gig with Kings Swing and also my temporary road census job.

Kings Swing were totally miffed that I was leaving them as I was too much an integral part of the band for them to continue without me - they had no option but to disband. They obviously tried to persuade me to stay saying that with them I was the star, but with Tommy I was just one of the band. I must admit that it wasn't an easy decision, but I decided to go back with Tommy. I didn't want to be a star anyway; I just enjoyed the buzz of playing with incredible musicians.

The final gig with Kings Swing was at the Windmill Club attached to Rotherham football club and was exceptional. It was announced that this was to be our last gig and the compere commented that he couldn't understand why a group as good as ours should be breaking up. Then I was collected from that gig by a friend of Tommy's and taken straight to where they were working which as it happened was also in Rotherham - the Oasis. I remember one of the audience asking Tommy's friend, "Where are you taking him?" To which he replied, "Back to where he belongs!"

Emile Ford - an incredible coincidence!

Before the next night's performance with Tommy, I did my last late afternoon with the road census team so as not to let them down, even though it was going to be a bit of a rush for me to get to the club in Rotherham. I didn't collect my months wages from them until six months later and they thought I'd died.

During the census we just had to stop about one in every four or five vehicles and ask them where they'd come from and where they were going and why.

I pulled this guy in and asked him the questions and he said he'd driven up from London to go to the Oasis club to see the Tommy Hunt band. I must admit I was a bit stunned. I told him that I play with them and I'll see him later. He must have thought I was a nutter. Why would I be working on a road census if I was working with Tommy Hunt a couple of hours later? Maybe he thought I was a delinquent doing community service or something. Anyway, he turned out to be Emile Ford who I'd never heard of. But apparently, he had the last UK No. 1 of the 50's and first of the 60's with "What do you wanna make those eyes at me for?"

I thought he must be a mate of Tommy's, but as it happened, he didn't want to see Tommy, he wanted to see us, the band as he'd just recorded a new single and wanted us to back him on some TV shows.

This didn't interfere with what we did with Tommy as they were all daytime so we agreed and the following week we were doing these TV performances with Emile. As Roger was no longer with us, we got a guy called Bernie to stand in. Bernie was the resident bass player at the Oasis club and could do remarkable Benny Hill interpretations as well as playing bass.

One of the TV's was Pebble Mill at One in Birmingham, and this one was *'live'* whereas the others were recorded and shown on later dates. We arrived as arranged, got set up and waited for Emile. Five minutes before we were due on, Emile had still not arrived, so the producer said, "Ok lads you'll have to do something on your own." Had we had Roger on bass this would have been no problem at all as there were several good instrumentals that we could have done. But all we could do with Bernie was Tommy's show and what we did with Emile. But the producer insisted that we'd better think of something quick because we were on in five minutes - *'live'!*

We didn't have time to rehearse anything, so we just had time to talk about what we could do. We'd agreed to do something that we all knew, but for some reason Bernie insisted on doing it in E flat, while I knew it in E. Transposing up or down a semitone on guitars is easy as you've just got to shove everything up or down a fret. But on keyboards transposing in your head is a different ball game as there's a stack of flats and sharps to contend with. I don't mind admitting that I was shitting myself.

Then the presenter's introduction went something like this: "Well we were going to have Emile Ford and the Checkmates for you today, but unfortunately Emile Ford has been held up, so here's the Checkmates - oh hang on Emile's just arrived, he's just taking his coat off!" And with that, we started playing his intro, he was thrown a microphone and all was well, and I breathed a sigh of relief.

I just wish I could get hold of a copy of that recording. It must be somewhere in the BBC archives. I have tried but so far haven't got anywhere.

Many trips over the Snake Pass

Most of the gigs with Tommy were in the North and I was able to commute from Sheffield every day. Although sometimes it did get a bit hard as quite a few were in or near Liverpool which was a fair trot. But whichever way I went to the West I had to negotiate either the Snake or the Woodhead Pass across the Pennines, both of which in those days were potentially dangerous and it could be icy or snowing there when it was perfectly fine in Sheffield and Manchester.

As there were no mobile phones, if you broke down or had an accident you were very much reliant on other motorists for help; but at 3:00 am they were few and far between. The only other contact with civilization on the Snake was an AA telephone box midway and possibly the Snake Inn, but you'd probably have died of hypothermia before getting to either. On the Woodhead there was nowhere.

If you hit a patch of black ice on a bend and didn't deal with it correctly, you'd have been over the edge and it would have been 'Goodnight Vienna', *and your carcass probably wouldn't have been found for a fortnight!*

I remember one night leaving Manchester at 3:00 am and arriving back in Sheffield at 10:00 am due to digging myself out of the snow on the Snake and it wasn't even snowing in Sheffield. Just me, the car, the snow and a shovel - sometimes it felt a bit lonely and scary. Whenever I could I'd always pick up any available hitchhikers to keep me company.

But it wasn't just snow, sometimes the fog was horrendous. Another time both the Snake and the Woodhead passes were closed and I had to use the M62, but the fog was so bad I could only just see the end of the bonnet, so obviously (to me) I reduced speed accordingly. Unfortunately, not everyone else did. I heard lorries thundering up behind me and slamming their brakes on at the last second when they saw my fog lights - *very frightening!*

So as soon as I reached the services which seemed to take forever, I pulled in and stayed until daylight. In a similar circumstance today, you'd get charged or fined for staying at the services for more than two hours, that's assuming there was room for you to stop anyway - *more modern day 'progress' I guess!*

Also, during this time just about all the petrol stations were giving away a free glass with every gallon of petrol. With the miles that I was clocking up I had glasses popping out of my earholes!

And of course, I got stopped by the police *at least* once or twice or more every night without fail, just for a routine check to find out what I was doing driving in the middle of the night - never a problem, just a bit irritating. One night I was followed by an unmarked police car all the way from Glossop and they virtually took my car apart when I arrived back in Sheffield, presumably looking for drugs which weren't there. I knew the car behind me was the police as I kept within the speed limits rigorously and they stayed behind me even at 2:00 am, anyone else would have overtaken me.

Sheffield Fiesta with Buddy Rich

The Sheffield Fiesta was the largest and probably best nightclub / cabaret club in Europe. Huge acts from all over the world performed there. Even Elvis Presley was in negotiations to perform there, but unfortunately that never came to fruition. But nevertheless, the Fiesta put Sheffield on the map!

One of my most memorable gigs with Tommy was one time that we worked at the Fiesta. We were topping the bill for five nights and jazz drummer Buddy Rich with his band were topping for the final two nights. So we had two days off (paid) and free *'ringside'* tables to see Buddy Rich.

During one of his performances there was a heckler, to which Buddy said, "Are you a drummer?" The reply was, "Yes." Then Buddy said, "Well why aren't you working?" *That shut him up!*

Out of all the acts I've ever seen he certainly rated as one of the best. And what a great environment to see him in. The huge arenas of today are so impersonal, but the Fiesta was perfect, I really can't understand why the Fiesta and similar venues closed down - *progress, I guess!* But so much of the progress over the last fifty years has been backwards.

At the time there was a big thing going about who was the best drummer Buddy Rich or Ginger Baker. I've had the pleasure of seeing both *'live'* and I can't see what the big argument was about. They were both incredible, but also very different. I certainly couldn't say that one was better than the other. *At the time they were both the best in the world!*

The Double Diamond Club Caerphilly

Another particularly memorable gig for me was when we worked at the Double Diamond Club in Caerphilly and my cousin Gary and his wife Beth came to see us. Gary (RIP) was the only family member to ever see me perform professionally apart from Janet and one of her sisters. I guess the distances were always a problem.

The next day Tex and I drove to Llwydcoed and had lunch with Gary's mum (Auntie Bec).

My last gig with Tommy

Coming up on Tommy's gig list were many weeks down south where I would have been unable to commute. So, about a month before this I told him I was leaving, but I don't think he believed me or just wouldn't accept it. The last gig I did with him was the Aquarius in Chesterfield. At the end of the last evening the band were pleading with me to stay and Janet was pleading with me to stay in Sheffield. Tommy just kept offering me more and more money, but it wasn't about money. I have to admit, it was a very difficult decision which tore me to pieces. I loved the band and the music but not the lifestyle. Chris Holmes who I took over from eventually took back over from me. And the bass player from the disbanded King's Swing took over on bass on my recommendation, how long for I've no idea.

On the way back to Sheffield at about 2:00 am my exhaust pipe bracket broke causing me to pull into a layby in the middle of nowhere. A police patrol man pulled in to find out what I was doing there. He then kindly crawled under the car in the rain and did a temporary fix for me. *Can you imagine that happening today?*

Cindy's

So next I needed to find myself a gig in Sheffield. Well, Janet found out about a new basement club / restaurant due to open in Sheffield to be called Cindy's. This was owned by a guy called Rod Trueman and his wife Cindy.

It wasn't huge so it was to be expensive and exclusive. After meeting with Rod, I was asked to form a band and Janet got a job there waitressing.

I pinched the resident drummer from the Sheffield Cavendish club (can't remember his name but he was good) and found a good singer guitarist called Barry Marshall. The budget didn't stretch to a bass player which I was a bit miffed about. I would have preferred a bass player to a guitarist. But Barry was a good singer / guitarist and compensated for the lack of bass wherever he could but it certainly wasn't ideal. Barry was very much into David Gates, so we did a lot of his stuff, plus quite a few organs based instrumentals.

Rod managed to acquire a top chef and the place was looking good. Although the place had a great bar, it was a licensed restaurant only, which meant that you had to buy a meal in order to buy a drink.

Everything plodded on ok for a few weeks, but although the place was busy and the food was very good, the name of the game was profit and the figures didn't add up.

Rod also had a row of small shops which he ran very profitably, but he might have been a bit out of his league with Cindy's. Clearly, he had to change tactics.

Firstly, he started opening at lunchtimes for *'business lunches'* and one day he got his wife Cindy to do some *'exotic'* dancing as we played. Unexpectedly to us she did a striptease which clearly went down well with the audience. *Rod then knew he was onto a winner!*

Bring on the strippers

So, Rod brought in a load of stripper's, sacked the chef, got Janet in the kitchen cooking egg and chips *'en mass'* and charged an entrance fee to include the compulsory egg and chips. This then enabled the punters to drink all night without contravening the licensing laws.

Although he was clearly within the law, the council weren't happy and were hell bent on closing him down. Personally, I couldn't see why as the place was jam packed every night, everyone was happy and there was never any trouble. Everyone was a winner! *Even the council got their bloody business rates for goodness sake!*

Some of these strippers incidentally came with a variety of paraphernalia, often huge pythons. I was always a bit worried that one of these beasts would jump off them onto me, but thankfully they never did. They obviously got a kick out wriggling around naked female bodies - *understandable, I guess!*

But it always used to confuse me as to why these girls seemed to think they needed to do anything more than strip off. One used to strip off and then do a naked fire eating act! *Baffling!* Once you'd got passed the screams of "Show us yer tits", and the rest came off, that's all the punters were interested in - *not a bloody fire eating act!*

As a way of supplementing the girls' incomes, Barry and I used to auction off what they took off at the end of the evenings. So, some poor sod would go home to his wife pissed out of his brains with a pair of sweaty knickers in his pocket that he'd just paid about fifty quid for! I must admit I feel a little guilty about that.

As time went by things did get a bit raunchy and the council were even more determined to close the place down. So, Rod asked us (the band) to ask the strippers exactly what they were going to do and inform them that they mustn't do anything obscene. I remember Barry asking one girl this and she said, "Do you mind if I make love to my pet fox?" Well Barry looked at me and said, "Is that obscene?" I must add that this was a stuffed fox, not a real one, but she stripped off and did it anyway.

Next, plain clothed police were in there every night for about a month gathering evidence of the goings on and sadly the place was eventually closed down which was a shame. No doubt the police gathering the evidence enjoyed their work and dragged it on for as long as they possibly could!

Sadly, Cindy died far too young and Rod went on to run a guest house in Blackpool. They were both genuinely lovely people and good friends.

Moving on

To be honest although Cindy's was a bit of a laugh it was also a big bring down musically for me and to say that I was disillusioned was an understatement.

I then received an offer from Chipperfield's circus to join them (playing the organ, not lion training, but I'm sure the wife could have done that with no trouble), but I just couldn't see myself playing all that circus music, so I declined even though they put on a great deal of pressure.

Then almost by accident I fell into driving instructing and packed up music at least temporarily. I could only do two things - play keyboards and drive! As a result of packing up music I didn't play or listen to music for several years as it depressed me so much. I didn't want to be watching it or listening to it, I wanted to be playing it!

I just immersed myself into the driving school and built one of the largest most successful schools in South Yorkshire, as well as a driving school supplies business. I can't say that I didn't enjoy driving instructing as I met some wonderful people over the years from many different cultures, several of whom became good lifelong friends. But I sadly lost contact with all my music friends at least temporarily. If truth be known I guess I felt guilty packing in music when I was riding high. Was it the right decision? I don't know. *Who knows what life has in store for us?*

I've taught doctors, nurses, lawyers, teachers, miners, steel workers, firemen, builders and every profession you can think of - even a rat catcher; Chinese, Muslims, Hindus, Sikhs, Jews, Buddhists, Sufis, Rastafarians, Christians and atheists. I've been to Muslim and Hindu weddings, Rastafarian parties, Sikh temples, and been given presents of different foods from just about everywhere - *my philosophy on gifts has always been that if I can't eat it or drive it, I don't want it!* They've all been lovely people. All of them basically wanted to live in peace, which makes me realise that all the trouble in the world is stirred up by politicians and powermongers - not the *normal* people of *any* culture!

The Full Monty

At first there was plenty of business as Sheffield was booming with the steel works and the mines etc. But then came the recession when most of the steel works closed down as in the Full Monty film. The knock-on effect was felt by every business large and small and then of course to make matters worse all the mines were shut down too. *Sheffield had it hard for a long, long time!*

During this period, it was particularly difficult for all driving schools and many went bust. But I was determined to succeed which I did. Part of my success was due to changing to Minis which appealed to most of the young women - particularly at the Northern General nurses' home where I built up a virtual monopoly. I worked long and hard from early mornings till late at night. Looking back, I don't know how I did it - 8:00 am till 8:00 pm on the driving school, then I built the driving school supplies business in the late evenings, sometimes till 2:00 am. But there were also times when I couldn't work due to snow and ice. One year it went on for months continuously, so I had to learn to *'make hay when the sun shined'!*

I must admit that I feel a tad guilty at being partially responsible for increasing the amount of traffic on our already crowded roads, but if it wasn't me, it would have been somebody else.

Unbelievably 30 years went by in a flash. Then after a load of grief from the taxman - brought to a close thanks to my dad's accountant Adrian John to whom I remain eternally grateful, I sold both businesses and retired to Cyprus aged 54 where we had a lovely villa custom built with a pool and all the trimmings. My driving school is still operating even today under my name, currently owned by one of the instructors who used to work for me.

Cyprus

Whilst in Cyprus I did take up playing again and had a gig on my own in a really nice restaurant in Paphos called The Almond Tree, a far cry from the Sheffield Fiesta but I enjoyed it nonetheless. I also did a few other gigs all of which were enjoyable. Additionally, I started a small sign making business - guess I just couldn't stop working. I once sold a vehicle sign to a guy who made blinds which read, "A blind man drives this van!" *I bet he got a stack of grief from that!*

But although I loved Cyprus there were downsides. For me it was just too hot in the summer months even floating in the pool. And of course, the swimming pool needed cleaning and the chemicals balancing every day 365 days a year. For anyone wanting a swimming pool, I'd recommend using salt water as they are less maintenance and don't need all the chemicals - *but I guess they could possibly attract a bunch of passing sharks!*

I also came across quite a few snakes, tarantulas and, scorpions (evil little bastards), that's not to mention the cockroaches and the mosquitos which they never tell you about in all the brochures. But as much as I tried, I never saw a ruddy mouflon. If you don't know, a mouflon is a type of wild sheep with *'handles'* only found in Cyprus, Turkey and thereabouts.

The illusive Mouflon

I spent days up in the mouflon country looking for the damned elusive beasts with camera ready, but to no avail, and during that time it also reminded me how much I missed the beautiful Derbyshire and Welsh countryside. In my head I couldn't help comparing the scenery to home, and Derbyshire and Wales always came out winning - *even in the rain!*

Whilst there I got to know an Indian restauranteur who I made a few signs for. He once said to me, "Are you working today", I replied, "No, it's Sunday", - "Well you should be, you're a bloody immigrant now just like me!" I know he was joking, but he was right - I *was* a bloody immigrant. It sounds stupid, but I no longer felt like I could ever truly belong there.

And in truth beyond all the phoney baloney hugs and kisses there was an underlying degree of animosity between the locals and the ex-pat immigrants - particularly with the number of swimming pools using their valuable water recourses which I can fully understand, even though the water was paid for. In fact, if you went up the hill to Kathikas above Peyia where we lived, you could often look down onto a cloud caused by all the swimming pools evaporating, all of which then got topped up! I must admit I thought ours was leaking at first with the amount it needed topping up, but it was just evaporation.

But I would certainly recommend Cyprus to anyone for a holiday. The temperature is agreeable for holidays all year round, although February is probably the worst month. It's generally safe to walk the streets any time of the day or night. There are ancient artifacts on virtually every street corner, as well as some hidden gems like the Adonis falls and the Akamas peninsula - *but you need a 4x4 for both!* And if you've never had fried halloumi cheese with tomatoes in pitta bread, you really must try it! - And they've even got some proper tea shops - *run by Brits of course!*

It's said that it's possible to go skiing in the Troodos mountains, sunbathing on the beach, and swimming in the sea all on the same day. Well just to prove this point I once tried it, although I don't ski personally (I've only got two legs and want to keep both), we went to Mount Olympus in Troodos and saw people skiing, then returned to Paphos to sunbathe and swim - so I know it's true but probably only in the winter when there's snow in the hills! And to be honest the ski runs look very basic and certainly wouldn't compare to the Alps or even Scotland. Another good thing about Cyprus is that most of them drive on the left - *but you have to keep a keen eye out for the others!*

But one particularly annoying thing about Cyprus is that there's three different prices in many restaurants (never listed on the menu):

- One for the tourists (menu price) and they'd never know any different.

- One for the ex-pats and

- One for the locals (lowest)

Well at least we reached ex pat status! And if you don't know the meaning of the word *'nepotism'*, you'd soon find out if you lived in Cyprus! *While we were there a couple expat businesses mysteriously burnt down and nothing was done about it!*

Although I'm very grateful and feel privileged for the time we had in Cyprus and for the beautiful villa, we decided to return to the UK mainly because of the heat and partly because we saw quite a few elderly people there who were desperate to go home and couldn't sell. Several of our ex pat friends also sold up and returned home at the same time as us for the same reasons.

Our Villa in Peyia, Cyprus

We enjoyed many great times with all our ex pat friends over there with regular get-togethers which we missed very much when we returned to the UK.

Remarkably we sold our villa, car and the small sign business that I'd started all within a week of a return flight to Manchester which we'd booked six months previously (originally as a holiday flight). Actually, I worked on doing this but that's another story - *and we didn't even use an agent!*

Apparently, the average British immigrants stay for three years before returning to the UK, and that's exactly how long we stayed despite thinking we were there for keeps.

We then put our furniture in storage, bought a tent on eBay which we picked up just outside Manchester airport, lived in that for a fortnight then bought a large Hymer motorhome with a car on a trailer and toured around Britain for six months before buying a bungalow in Lincolnshire; but later we returned to Sheffield where I now write keyboard tuition books which thankfully are selling well.

Often, we take a drive over the Woodhead pass to Glossop and return via the Snake - it really is food for the soul, I just never get fed up with it whatever the weather! And it also reminds me of many of my musical journeys. And sometimes we go to Derwent valley on Christmas day to feed the ducks when it's deserted - *apart from the ducks of course!*

The Peak District is beautiful, but don't go telling everyone as it's already starting to get a bit crowded!

Janet still likes to go to France and Spain, which we do in our caravan, but personally I've absolutely no desire to go further south than Bakewell, *where I've got a thing going with the local tart!*

The Great Cyprus bank robbery

No, the bank didn't get robbed, the bank robbed the customers - *badly!* In 2012, not all that long after we returned to the UK the bank of Cyprus had a financial crisis and decided to solve it by seizing its customers assets. In fact, 47.5% of investors assets over €100,000 were literally, and allegedly legally, *'stolen'*. Had we still been there and had our money in the wrong bank (not every bank was affected) we could have lost over £100,000 which would have been totally gut wrenching. You could understand that sort of thing going on in Robin Hood's time, but now? I can certainly appreciate why many people keep all their assets in cash or gold!

If you can't trust the governments and banks, who can you trust? Your solicitor?

We had one solicitor who ended up being a double murderer (and he seemed such a nice man); he eventually surrendered whilst hanging onto a gargoyle on Amiens cathedral 200' above the ground. Two others were imprisoned for embezzlement and one ran off to South Africa with over

£1,000,000 of a client's funds (all in Sheffield), another lost our house deeds and a few more were just total plonkers! Hence the saying that 99% of solicitors give the rest a bad name.

Bring back the good old days! The days of honesty and decency. When you could walk the streets without fear and when politicians of all the parties were in the job for the good of the country and not to feather their own nests!

Where is everyone now?

With the arrival of the internet, I managed to rekindle my friendships with many of my old band buddies but sadly many have died.

Tapestry

Unfortunately, I've not been able to trace the whereabouts of most of the original Tapestry members, which is a great shame as Mike Hutson and Pete Frolich were both great friends. But I do know that David Moses went on to write books about recorders which he was very much into even back then. He's also done a fair bit of work for the BBC children's TV. See: https://tinderboxmusic.co.uk for his website.

Ralph - Aquila

After Aquila, so far as I know Ralph didn't perform again but went on to write a very successful guitar book. He continued living at Hendon and when Alistair died, he bequeathed the house to Ralph. Sadly, Ralph died in 2011 way before his time, but his book lives on and is still selling well even today.

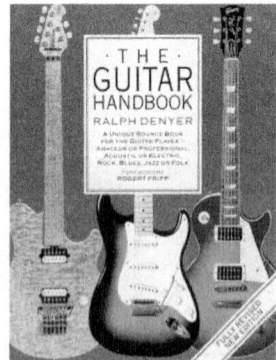

Jim - The Fantastics, Aquila & Geno

After Geno, Jim got divorced from Myja which didn't surprise me. I don't think Myja ever really came to terms with the fact that Jim wasn't a mega star in the UK as he was in Poland. He then worked with a US soul band in Benidorm for a summer season and got ripped off very badly. Totally disillusioned he threw away his drum sticks then made a living buying and selling cars for a while before starting a very successful computer programming business. He later remarried, moved to Brighton and had a daughter very late in life. He told me that he just wanted to live long enough to protect his daughter from all the randy young males! Sadly, Jim passed on in September 2023, but I'm so glad that Jim, George, Ronnie and I got to meet up before then.

Jim with his young daughter Emma-Christina

Phil - Aquila

After Aquila, Phil worked with several more bands including: Elkie Brooks, Lulu and the Opus One Big Band which was a Glen Miller Tribute band. Sadly, Phil also passed onto the other side before I got to see him again.

George - Aquila

After Aquila, George worked with a few London based soul and jazz bands and is a regular at all the popular London jam sessions. Being a family man, he no longer wished to tour any more. George is a truly talented musician as well as being a lovely person and a good friend.

Spam - The Fantastics

Spam (Pete Cole) went on to have a couple of hit records in the Caribbean with Joyce Bond, as well as playing with several other bands throughout the world. He also wrote a couple of successful books about Goldfish. The last time I contacted him; he was living in a château in the South of France and was still as mad as ever.

Ronnie - The Fantastics

After the Fantastics, Ron worked with Tommy Hunt (but before I was with him) and then with The Heavy Metal Kids which continued for several years. He now lives in Brighton not far from where Jim lived.

Pip - The Fantastics

After a stunt playing with Jimmy James and the Vagabonds, Pip went on to be a top session musician and record producer. He's produced hundreds of hit records, but probably best known for his work with Status Quo, the Moody Blues, the Sweet, Mud, and Barbara Dickson. For many years I had no idea what Pip was up to, then one day in 2008 I heard him on the radio with Barbara Dickson. I'm now back in touch with him.

I remember Pip saying many years ago in the van that he wanted to get into producing, well he certainly did and good on him! His success was well earned! A great guy. I've never heard him say a bad word about anyone!

Pip in the studio displaying one of his well-earned awards!

Roger - Geno & Tommy Hunt

I'm regularly in touch with Roger. Even though he's older than me, he's still gigging, currently with the Swinging Blue Jeans - *I don't know how he stays awake!*

Roger has also made three brilliant albums of his own, two of which are contemporary Christian.

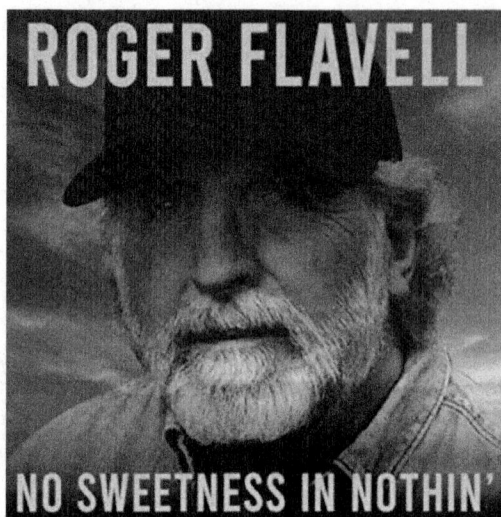

Roger's 3rd solo Album

After Tommy, among others Roger worked with Christie (Yellow River), The Byron Band, The Lonnie Donegan Band, The Orchestra pit at the Hexagon Theatre in Reading (mainly pantomimes) and the Blue Jeans. He also now writes children's books. A truly multi-talented person as well as being a lovely man and great friend. See http://rogerflavell.co.uk.

Tex - Tommy Hunt

After Tommy, Tex played with White Plains, Joe Brown, Robin Box, Pete Sayers, and No Spring Chicken. Tex is still rocking on! *We had so much fun together!*

Kevan - Tommy Hunt

After Tommy, Kevan worked and recorded with Charles Aznavour. I have to say that this gig no doubt suited him perfectly! Sadly, Kevan died too early in Florida in 2010.

Alan Simonds - From the Beginning

Alan never turned pro as a musician despite his talents, but continued working in electronics until he took a job lecturing on computers at a college in West Sussex. Later he moved to France and started a web design business but has since retired and returned to the UK. I speak with Alan regularly. During a lifetime you don't get many friends from beginning to end such as Alan has been to me.

Martin Tottle - From the Beginning

Martin performed professionally for a few years but packed in due to family commitments. He's still married to his original girlfriend Marilyn who I knew from way back. He's since changed his surname to Johnstone. Thankfully we are still in touch on a regular basis.

Brother Steve - From the Beginning

It's funny how one event in life leads to another, then another and another etc. And if the first event never occurred, all the others couldn't have either! So, I guess if Steve hadn't bought his first guitar, none of the following events would have occurred, and Aquila would never have existed. *So, thanks Steve!*

Although we argued like cat and dog in the early days, we've always been the best of friends!

Steve never turned pro as a guitarist despite eventually becoming an excellent player. He just continued in his career in electronics. But to be honest the lifestyle would not have suited him as his comfort zone is only within a ten-mile radius of his house. *But he's happy!*

Obviously I see Steve whenever I can and we talk regularly on the phone.

Steve - Picture taken by younger brother, Glyn

Reunions

John Cheatdom

My first reunion was with John Cheatdom in the early 80's although it wasn't planned. By chance we went to see the Platters at the Leadmill club, Sheffield and low and behold John was singing with them.

Afterwards, I saw their roadie and told him that I used to work with John and would like to say hello to him. He told me that there's no-one of that name in the group and I must be mistaken. It turned out that they were trying to kid everyone on that he was one of the original Platters! There was actually only one of the originals at the time, but to be fair they were very good.

I said, "Look, I lived and worked with that guy for a year, so I know exactly who is, now go and tell him." Moments later I was ushered down into the dressing room. John of course remembered me and was pleased to see me. He introduced me to the rest of the group and said that we were without doubt the best Fantastics backing band. But all the phoney baloney dressing room crap from everyone else who managed to get there really took me back and annoyed me, and I couldn't wait to get out of there. But John was a great guy and it was good to see him again! That was the last I saw of any of the Fantastics.

Alan Simonds

I speak regularly with Alan back from the very early days and met him both in France when he lived there and again in Seaford when he returned to the UK.

Me and Alan at his place in France.

Jim, Ronnie and George

With me living in Sheffield and everyone else living down south, meeting up has been difficult. But in May 2019 four of us did manage to get together in East Grinstead when I was on the way to France and Spain with our caravan.

George from Aquila came down from London on the train and Jim (from the Fantastics, Aquila and Geno) and Ronnie (from the Fantastics) drove up from Brighton together. It would have been wonderful if Pip was there too but unfortunately, he couldn't make it due to health issues, but I am back in touch with him.

L-R George, me & Jim

We had a truly great afternoon reminiscing about past events and catching up on what we'd all done later.

Sadly, Jim has now passed on leaving me and George the only two surviving members of Aquila, and me, Pip, Spam and Ronnie the surviving members of the Fantastics' band.

L-R Ronnie, me & Jim

Roger Flavell

In late November 2023 I managed to meet up with Roger in Sheffield when he was gigging at the City Hall with Blue Jeans. Although it was incredible to see Roger again in person after over fifty years, it came with a spooky experience.

We arranged to meet outside the City Hall at about 5:30. I remember meeting him at that time and then going to a nearby Café Nero. We both had a drink and Roger had a sandwich as he hadn't eaten for a while - *life on the road really buggers up your eating habits!* Then the café was closing so we went to another Café Nero a few blocks away which was open until later, then............. I totally lost my memory which wasn't apparent to Roger or me at the time. It's crazy but I didn't even remember not remembering.

Roger (left) and me 2023

Apparently, we had another drink at the second café, then I walked with Roger back to the City Hall where I took the selfie photo of us both before saying our goodbyes. In fact, I don't even remember going to the second café or taking the photo. The next thing I remembered was waking up in bed in the middle of the night a bit confused and looking out of the bedroom window wondering where the car was.

So I'm told, after I left Roger I walked back to the second café and just sat there. After a while the staff in the café became concerned about me and got hold of my mobile phone. Presumably they checked recent numbers and called our youngest son who was hundreds of miles away. I couldn't remember who I was, where I'd been or where my car was parked (which was probably a good thing). My son called Janet and arranged an Uber taxi to collect her and come and get me. The following morning, I still remembered nothing of the previous evening after initially meeting Roger. But I had a good idea where I'd probably parked the car, so we went and retrieved that before going to the doctor.

The doctor did all sorts of tests including blood tests and found nothing wrong. There was incidentally no trace of any drugs or alcohol in my system, which I was 100% sure there wouldn't have been. Shortly after, I spoke with Roger several times who helped me try to piece everything together, but I only managed to remember small bits of when I was with him then absolutely nothing after.

The most probable thing that it appears to have been is something called 'Transient Global Amnesia' which thankfully is just a one-off event and rarely recurs, but it's nevertheless quite worrying. Perhaps after seeing Roger after so long, it blew a fuse in my brain. It's probably just as well that I didn't find my car as I might have started driving back down the M1 to London.

Or............*maybe I was abducted by aliens and they chucked me back out as a reject!*

In Closing

I'm truly thankful for the amazing memories of those exciting times and the buzz of playing with so many incredible musicians.

And finally, I'd like to thank you sincerely for buying this book. It's been my sincere desire to provide more value in real terms than the cost of this book. I hope that you think that I've succeeded, if so your positive feedback on Amazon or Lulu etc., would be very much appreciated!

For my sins, Lilly (below) has been sent up from the depths of Hell to torment me for the rest of my days!

Lilly, my loveable tormentor!

Wishing you Good Health, Wealth and Wisdom,

Martin

Other books by Martin Woodward

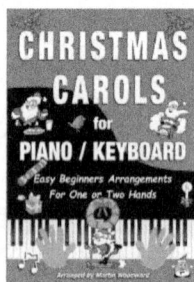

See: https://learn-keyboard.co.uk (or scan the QR code) for details of the above and more.

Printed in Dunstable, United Kingdom

73805835R00080